THE
Good
Witch's
DAILY
SPELLBOOK

FALL RIVER PRESS

New York

An Imprint of Sterling Publishing Co., Inc.
1166 Avenue of the Americas
New York, NY 10036

ISBN 978-1-4351-6345-4

Distributed in Canada by Sterling Publishing Co., Inc.
c/o Canadian Manda Group, 664 Annette Street
Toronto, Ontario, Canada M6S 2C8
Distributed in the United Kingdom by GMC Distribution Services
Castle Place, 166 High Street, Lewes, East Sussex, England BN7 1XU
Distributed in Australia by NewSouth Books
45 Beach Street, Coogee, NSW 2034, Australia

For information about custom editions, special sales, and premium
and corporate purchases, please contact Sterling Special Sales at
800-805-5489 or specialsales@sterlingpublishing.com.

Manufactured in China

2 4 6 8 10 9 7 5 3 1

www.sterlingpublishing.com

Book design by Sharon Leigh Murray Jacobs

THE
Good
Witch's
DAILY
SPELLBOOK

Quick, Simple, and Practical Magic for Every Day of the Year

Patti Wigington

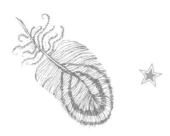

Introduction

Have you ever stopped to think about how much you'd like to change some of the different aspects of your life? Maybe you wish you were luckier in love. Perhaps you'd like to see your career take off. You might be someone whose needs and wants are along more spiritual lines than material ones—have you ever hoped to improve your levels of wisdom or intuition, or maybe wanted to delve into a bit of psychic protection for your family?

Even more important, at some point, you may just have stopped to think *I wish there was a magic spell for this…*

Guess what?

There probably is.

Throughout recorded history, people of every religious background have embraced the use of magic to bring about change and transformation in their lives. While many people include their religion as part of their magical practice, that's not what this book is about. *The Good Witch's Daily Spellbook* is about practical magic—spellwork that has tangible effects. If you want to incorporate your spiritual beliefs as you're working your way through this book, you're certainly welcome, but it's specifically designed so you don't have to.

Let's talk a bit about some basics you need to keep in mind before we get started.

Magic, Month by Month

THE GOOD WITCH'S DAILY SPELLBOOK is set up so you can effectively work a different spell each day of the year. From January's themes of new beginnings to December's focus on wrapping up the winter darkness, there's a different one for you to try each day. Ideally, you'll use this book every year, which is why you may have to make a few adjustments of your own. For example, there are thirteen moon spells, evenly spaced four weeks apart (with two appearing in January), for a variety of seasonal purposes. Because the full moon dates vary from year to year, you don't necessarily have to do them on the date they appear in this book. The same goes for days like the equinoxes and solstice dates—they're not always the same, so tweak your agical calendar accordingly.

Likewise, February 29 appears as a birthday spell. However, we all know that February has twenty-nine days only every four years, which means the birthday spell is a magical bonus round. Use it whenever your birthday actually falls, at any time of year.

Many magical traditions today assign meanings and characteristics to the different days of the week. If you want to use these, you can, but not everyone does.

If you need to do a money spell on Sunday afternoon, don't feel obligated to wait until Thursday—do it when it makes the most sense for you. For those of you who do want to assign weekday correspondences to your spellwork, here is a general guideline you can use:

SUNDAY
Healing, spiritual success, protection, and strength.

MONDAY
Peace, dreams and sleep, intuition, and purification.

TUESDAY
Battle and conflict, passion, and sex.

WEDNESDAY
Studying and learning, wisdom, and communication.

THURSDAY
Prosperity and abundance, money, and generosity.

FRIDAY
Love, beauty, friendship, and reconciliation.

SATURDAY
Security, stability, longevity, and the home.

Last, but certainly not least, if you're part of a magical tradition that requires you to cast a circle, create sacred space, or call upon deity before any working, then go ahead and do it—but keep in mind that it's not necessary.

Your Magical Toolkit

A LOT OF PEOPLE COME into modern magical practice thinking they need to spend a bunch of money on a lot of supplies—candles in every color, herbs, seventeen different crystals, statues, goblets, fifty types of incense, and some other fancy trappings. I'm going to let you in on a little secret that every single good witch has figured out.

Are you ready?

You don't need a lot of stuff.

It's true! I know, it sounds crazy. You may *think* you do because a book or a website gave you a three-page list of things you need to have in your magical arsenal, but you really don't. You can do a lot of magic with things you already have around the house, and you can perform many of the spells in *The Good Witch's Daily Spellbook* with a minimal amount of financial investment.

If you absolutely feel like you must buy some supplies, your money is best spent on candles, because many of the spells in *The Good Witch's Daily Spellbook* involve candle magic. You don't need a lot and they don't have to be huge, but you might want to spend a few dollars on candles in the following colors:

4

RED
Courage, passion, and lust

ORANGE
Attraction and encouragement

YELLOW
Protection, empowerment, and persuasion

GREEN
Fertility, abundance, and prosperity

BLUE
Healing, understanding, and patience

PURPLE
Power and ambition

SILVER
Intuition, moon magic, and wisdom

GOLD
Money, solar magic, and power

BLACK
Banishing and negativity

WHITE
Purity and cleansing

In many magical traditions, white candles can be substituted for any other color. The best place to find a box of inexpensive white candles? Check the Kosher section at your grocery store for the box marked "Menorah Candles."

Making the Magic Happen

NO ONE KNOWS FOR SURE how or why magic works, and there are many different theories about the specifics. The important thing is that those of us who practice magical living know that it does work. Whether we've been practicing for three weeks or three decades, every spell cast is a learning experience. Just like learning to ride a bike or bake a cake, if you don't get the results you want the first time you cast a spell, it's perfectly okay to go back and do it again later.

You may find it beneficial to read through the entire book before you work a single spell. This will help you get a better idea of what kinds of things are included, and how they tie into the seasons and other agricultural markers. If a certain spell jumps out at you and you really want to try it, don't be afraid to give it a shot, even if it may not appear in *The Good Witch's Daily Spellbook* until several months from now.

Just like in all the nonmagical aspects of your life, practice makes perfect. With a bit of work and some focus, you can make all kinds of things happen in your life with magic. By the time you've done all 366 of them, you may not even think of yourself as a good witch at all. You might just be an *excellent* witch!

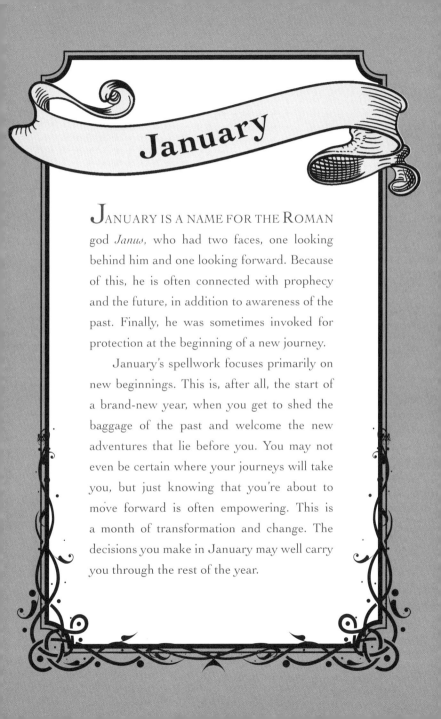

January

JANUARY IS A NAME FOR THE ROMAN god *Janus*, who had two faces, one looking behind him and one looking forward. Because of this, he is often connected with prophecy and the future, in addition to awareness of the past. Finally, he was sometimes invoked for protection at the beginning of a new journey.

January's spellwork focuses primarily on new beginnings. This is, after all, the start of a brand-new year, when you get to shed the baggage of the past and welcome the new adventures that lie before you. You may not even be certain where your journeys will take you, but just knowing that you're about to move forward is often empowering. This is a month of transformation and change. The decisions you make in January may well carry you through the rest of the year.

January 1

Spell for
New Beginnings

You'll need:
- A purple candle
- Your favorite incense

Are you ready to kick off the New Year? This is the season when many of us make resolutions, but sometimes, even with the best of intentions, it can be hard to stick to them. This spell is designed to kick-start your year of change and transformation. The purple candle represents empowerment and ambition.

Light the candle, and use the flame to light your incense. Take a moment to watch the smoke rise into the air. Think about all the places that smoke might end up going — and all the places you can go this year.

Consider all the opportunities you have to do things differently this year. Watch as the candle flame dances before you, and say, *It is a time for change. It is time to begin anew. It is time to be a new person, strong and secure and confident. These are the things I will achieve.*

List the things you will accomplish in the next twelve months, using active voice, rather than passive. Instead of saying *I wish I was healthier,"* say *I will be healthier.* Rather than *I would like to feel better about myself,* say *I will believe in myself and be confident.* Go on as long as you need to — and if you want to include mundane items like *I will get a new job,* then do it!

When you're done, blow out the candle, but let the incense burn away on its own.

January 2

Seed Divination Spell

You'll need:
- A silver candle
- Seven seeds or beans

The second day of January is associated with the Egyptian goddess Isis, who was—among many other things—a deity of magic. She's also connected to the season of planting and the early spring harvest in Egypt. Why not mark today by using seeds for a bit of divination, paired with a silver candle to aid your intuitive abilities?

Light the candle, and focus on what you hope to learn. After all, divination should have a purpose. Is your question related to love and relationships? Your job or education? Think about the specific purpose of your divination. When you're ready, close your eyes. Shake the seeds in your hands, and then—keeping your eyes shut—drop them on the table in front of you.

What shape do they form? Do you see a letter or number? An image of a heart or a dollar sign? Take a moment to figure out how the shape or image relates to your question.

If you're simply looking for a yes or no answer, use a piece of string as a dividing line. Assign one side of the line as yes and the other as no, and see which side the majority of the seeds land on.

January 3

Wolf Moon Spell to Banish Your Baggage

You'll need:
- A black candle
- A piece of paper and a pen
- A fireproof bowl

At the beginning of the New Year, it's always a good time to do a bit of self-evaluation. In some traditions of folklore, the first full moon of the year is known as the Wolf Moon. This is because, for our ancient ancestors, it was often the season when hungry wolves were howling outside the door. This simple spell will help you tap into a bit of lunar energy to help get rid of the things that might be dragging you down from last year. It's time to banish the wolves from your own door.

Try to perform this spell on the night of January's full moon, or on one of the three nights immediately afterward. Light the black candle. Think about all the baggage that has held you back, caused you problems, or made you feel unworthy. Write down these things, and then light the paper in the candle's flame. Place it in the bowl to burn, and as it does, say *Today, I say farewell to the things that have prevented me from becoming the person I wish to be. I send you away, far from me, and far from my life. You no longer have any influence upon me. You are my past, and the past is gone. I banish you, I banish you, I banish you.*

Once the paper has burned away to ashes, extinguish the candle. The next morning, bury the ashes someplace far away from your home.

January 4

Spell to Open the Door of Opportunity

You'll need:
• A piece of chalk • A door or gate

Janus, that Roman god whose name gives us *January*, is associated with gates and doorways. Some people believe that when one door closes, another one opens. The key is to recognize this when it happens. This spell will help create new opportunities for you in the coming year. Use an exterior door that leads into your home, or an interior door into various rooms in the house, depending on which aspect of your life you'd like to improve.

Stand on the opposite side of the door from the place you are about to enter—in other words, if the door enters your house, stand on the front step. Use the chalk to draw an outline around the edges of the door, going in a clockwise direction and tracing a circle around the knob. If the door includes windows, trace around them as well. As you do so, say *Opportunity knocks, and new doors open*, repeating it nine times as you trace the outline.

Once you've finished making your chalk outline, knock three times on the door, open it up, and let yourself in. Close it behind you, and on the inside of the door, use the chalk to draw an image of the success you hope to achieve. Hoping for a new love opportunity? Draw a heart. For financial success, draw dollar signs! Each time you enter that door, knock on it and repeat *Opportunity knocks, and new doors open*, and soon enough, you'll see the changes you're wishing for.

Make a Vision Board for Goal Setting

You'll need:
- Images representing your goals
- A piece of poster board
- Glue stick

Now is as good a time as any to set some new goals. Making a vision board is a great way to remind yourself of what you wish to manifest. Some people believe this method also attracts your desires and wants directly to you.

Lay out the images on the poster board. They should be pictures of things or concepts that you hope to achieve as part of your goal-setting process. Do you want that big promotion at work? Travel adventures? A happy family life in a nice house? Choose photos from magazines or online that really speak to your soul. Once you figure out how you want them arranged, glue them in place. As you do, repeat *I turn "I wish" into "I am," and the best is yet to come.*

Hang your vision board in a place where you'll see it every day, as a reminder of the goals you've set for this year.

January 6

Persephone
Spell for Protection

You'll need:
- A pomegranate

In classical mythology, Persephone was the daughter of Demeter, and she was trapped in the underworld with Hades for six months of every year. On January 6, her followers carried her statue around the temple, and invoked her for protection in the coming year. Persephone's symbol is the pomegranate, because it was her consumption of the seeds that led to her splitting time between the land of the living and that of the dead. If possible, do this working on a Sunday, which is associated with protection magic.

Open the pomegranate so you can access the seeds. Walk the perimeter of your property, dropping a seed at evenly spaced intervals. As you drop each seed, say *This home is protected, safe and secure. This land is protected, safe, and secure. All those who dwell here are protected, safe, and secure.*

Once you've dropped all the seeds, dig a small hole near your front door, and plant the skin and meat of the pomegranate.

Silver and Gold
Prosperity Magic

You'll need:
- A silver candle and a gold candle
- A piece of green paper
- A handful of pennies and dollar bills

This is the time of year when many of us are paying off our holiday expenses, so it's a great season to do a bit of prosperity magic. This basic money spell works on the very simple theory that like attracts like. Or, to put it simply, money attracts more money.

Light the candles, leaving enough space for you to work between them. Fold the piece of paper into an envelope or a pocket. As you do, say *Gold and silver, silver and gold, make money come and dollars unfold.*

Place the coins and bills into the envelope, and say *Pennies and paper, coins and ones, as I will, it shall be done.* Fold the top of the envelope closed and put it in a safe place where it will be undisturbed and out of sight. Blow out the candles when you're finished.

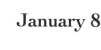

January 8

Justice
Spell

You'll need:
- Chamomile tea
  - Ginger root

The goddess Justitia represents the moral and fair forces of the justice system. January 8 was when she was invoked in tandem with the household gods to ensure swift and ethical resolution of court cases. If you're facing legal action, or you know someone who is, use this spell to guarantee an objective outcome. In folk magic, chamomile and ginger are associated with favorable legal findings.

The night before you appear in court, brew a pot of chamomile tea. Pour yourself a cup, and if you honor specific deities in your household, pour a cup for them as well. Drink the tea as the last thing you do right before you go to bed, and once the cup is empty, squeeze the excess moisture from the teabags, and place them under your pillow.

On the morning of the court appearance or trial, cut a small piece of ginger root to carry in your pocket as you go to the courthouse. Once you arrive, discreetly place it on the floor under your seat to bring about a fair and just decision.

January 9

Dream
Spell Pillow

You'll need:
- Blue fabric, about $\frac{1}{2}$ yard
- Cotton stuffing
- Dried lavender

It's easy to get stressed out during the darker half of the year, and the nights are long and cold in January. This is the perfect time to stitch up a magical pillow to bring about relaxing dreams. Lavender is associated with peacefulness and calm sleep. If possible, use blue fabric, which represents healing and tranquility. Try to do this working on a Monday, which corresponds to the moon and spellwork related to dreams.

Fold the fabric in half lengthwise, right sides together, and stitch around the three open sides, stopping when you still have an opening of about 4 inches. Turn the fabric inside out, so the pattern or design is on the outside. Stuff the pillow with the cotton filling and lavender. Stitch the hole closed, and as you do, say *When at night I go to sleep, sweet dreams will come to me. Lavender bring me peaceful rest, as I will so it shall be.*

January 10

Garnet Talisman
for Women's Ailments

You'll need:
- Your favorite incense or a scented candle
- Jeweler's wire
- A garnet stone
- A long necklace chain or leather thong

Garnet is the birthstone associated with the month of January, and it is tied to women's mysteries and maladies. Garnets are related to the root chakra and can be used in healing reproductive disorders and regulating the menstrual cycle. If you've been suffering from uncomfortable periods or cramps, or just feel a bit off-kilter during that time of the month, make this simple healing talisman using a garnet and some jeweler's wire.

Do this working once the sun has set. Find a quiet place to sit, and light some of your favorite incense or a scented candle. Use the jeweler's wire to wrap the garnet stone. Work slowly, imagining the energy of the garnet working its healing magic on your body. As you wrap the wire, say *Body and blood, healthy and whole. With garnet energy, pain be gone.*

Attach the wrapped stone to the chain or leather thong, and wear it around your neck when you start feeling symptoms. Note that a longer necklace is better because it allows the stone to hang closer to your reproductive organs.

January 11

Alphabet Divination

You'll need:
• A set of letter tiles,
like those used in word games
• A cloth bag

Carmenta was a goddess of divination and prophecy, and her name comes from the Latin *carmen*, which means a spell or song. Interestingly, as the English language evolved, it became the root of the word *charm*. Carmenta was credited with changing the Greek alphabet by altering the letters to form the new Latin language. Because she is associated with both divination and alphabets, January 11, the day of the Carmentalia festival, is a perfect time to combine these in your magical workings.

Place the tiles in the cloth bag, and start thinking about the question you want answered. Close your eyes, and one at a time withdraw nine tiles at random. Take a look. Do they spell out a name or word? Perhaps they illustrate a concept, like JOB or LOVE. If they don't seem to make sense, rearrange them until you see a message that applies to the question at hand. In some methods of rune interpretation, a blank rune indicates the hand of fate, so if you draw the blank letter tile, there could be forces at play that are out of your control.

January 12

Spell to Tie Up Your Problems

You'll need:
• A length of yarn, about 18 inches

With the sun setting early, and short hours of daylight, January is the time of year when many people focus on crafts related to domesticity and the home. Weaving, spinning, knitting, and other fiber arts are often associated with the dark winter months. If you have yarn handy—whether you spun it yourself or purchased it commercially—use a piece to get rid of the problems that may still be haunting you from last year.

Select your yarn color based on the problem at hand. Blue is for healing, red is for lust, white is for cleansing, and so on—refer to the section on color correspondences on page 5 for the full list. Beginning at one end, tie a knot in the yarn, visualizing the problem at hand. As you tie more and more knots, imagine the obstacle being tied up and rendered useless. Continue along the entire length of yarn until you can't tie any more. You should end up with a knotty, tangled mess. Take it somewhere away from your home, and bury it.

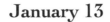

January 13

Midvintersblót Spell
for Friends and Family

You'll need:
- A bonfire
- A meal
- Friends and family

I n Sweden, January 13 is the festival of the *Midvintersblót*, the final day of the winter celebration of *Jul*. Historically, this was a time of both feasting and sacrifice. Food and hospitality rituals appear in a number of cultures, so celebrate the season by preparing a big meal for your friends and family, and wrap it up by making offerings together to strengthen your bond. Do this working after dark.

Light the fire and get a good roaring blaze going. As you eat your meal—preferably something you've cooked yourself, and involving lots of winter comfort food—ask your guests to save a bit of the food on their plates and the drinks in their cups. Once everyone has finished eating, invite each guest to join you in a circle around the fire.

One at a time, everyone throws their last bite of food and sip of drink into the flames. As each person adds his or her offering to the fire, the whole group can shout *We are family, we are kin, we are clan, we are blood, and we are bound by love and friendship!*

As the year progresses, try to get together regularly with the people you care about most.

January 14

Cat
Protection Spell

You'll need:
- A yellow candle
- A photo of your cat
- Catnip

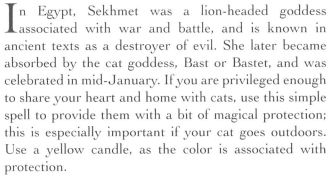

In Egypt, Sekhmet was a lion-headed goddess associated with war and battle, and is known in ancient texts as a destroyer of evil. She later became absorbed by the cat goddess, Bast or Bastet, and was celebrated in mid-January. If you are privileged enough to share your heart and home with cats, use this simple spell to provide them with a bit of magical protection; this is especially important if your cat goes outdoors. Use a yellow candle, as the color is associated with protection.

Light the candle, and place it beside the photo of your cat. Rub the catnip between your palms—this may bring your cat running in, and that's perfectly fine—until it becomes a fine powder. Sprinkle it around both the photo and the candle, forming a circle, and say *Great adventurer, wild warrior, noble cat, be protected on your journeys, within this home and in the wild. Wherever you roam, you will always return safe, healthy, and whole.*

Extinguish the candle when you are finished, or when your cat begins rolling around in the catnip dust.

21

January 15

Spell to Banish a Negative Person

You'll need:
- A black candle
- A piece of paper and a pen
- An envelope with a stamp

As the New Year begins, we often make the conscious effort to get rid of the negative things from our past. But what do you do when that negativity is coming from a *person*? Sometimes, a little magical boost is just the thing to make the negative, unhappy, soul-sucking individuals stay out of your life. This spell uses a black candle for banishing.

Light the candle, and write down the individual's name. Hold the paper in the candle's flame, burning away all the edges. As you do so, say *I banish your connection to me, I banish your feelings for me, I banish your ties to me, I banish your control over me.*

Stop when you get to the name itself. Put the remaining paper in the envelope, along with any ashes you may have accumulated, and mail it to the person, with no return address.

January 16

Harmonious Relationship Spell

You'll need:
- A red candle
- A piece of paper and a pen
- A red ribbon
- A small jar with a lid

Concordia was the classical goddess associated with harmonious marriages and relationships. In particular, she represents the possibilities that are open to two people who love each other in an equal, respectful partnership. Her festival was celebrated each year on January 16. If you've ever felt like your relationship has lost its spark, this is a perfect day to rebuild the harmony that you once felt. Try to do this working on a Friday, which is associated with the goddess Venus and her aspects of love and reconciliation.

Light the candle. Write down your name and your lover's name, as close together as possible, or even intersecting each other. Roll up the paper into a tight scroll, and tie it with the ribbon, as you say *Harmony, love, and passion's desire, it's time to rekindle our relationship's fire.*

Light one end of the paper from the candle flame, and place it in the jar. As it burns, focus on the harmony that you and your lover once had, and will it to return. After the flame burns out on its own, cap the jar and bury it in a part of your yard where you and your lover regularly go.

January 17

Good Luck Spell

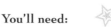

You'll need:
- A green ribbon
- A skeleton key

January 17 is the day dedicated to Fausta Felicitas, a goddess of good luck and fortune. If you want to increase your luck, this is a good day for magical workings. To unlock the good fortune that you want, use a skeleton key.

Thread the ribbon through the skeleton key, and knot it so you can wear it around your neck. Each time you put it on, say *Unlocking fortune with a simple key, good things plenty will come to me.*

January 18

Spell for
Unity and Peace

You'll need:
- A blue candle
- A packet of rosemary seeds
- A pot of soil and some water

On January 18, many people around the United States mark the anniversary of the birth of Martin Luther King, Jr., a man who worked tirelessly for equal rights by way of peaceful protest. This is a good day to do a spell for peace and unity. The blue candle and rosemary are associated with tranquility and healing. Rosemary takes a long time to germinate—sometimes as much as six weeks—so if you do this in January, you should have seedlings ready to transplant in the spring.

Light the candle, and take a moment to reflect on the need for peace in our world today. Is your focus global? A single country? Perhaps your local community needs help. Figure out where you want to direct your efforts. Press the rosemary seeds into the soil one at a time. As you do, say *Liberty, justice, freedom, peace, and unity. May all people find hope in times of despair, and light in the midst of darkness, coming together as one.*

Once you've planted all the seeds in the soil, add the water slowly, saying *May peace grow within our world, may hope grow within our world, may love grow within our world.*

After you have watered the soil, place the pot in a sunny window and water it regularly, so you can help the seeds of peace grow strong.

January 19

Cord Magic
to Stop a Gossip

You'll need:
• A 3-foot length of black cord

Ever encounter someone who just can't stop talking about things that shouldn't be his or her concern? We've all had these people in our lives, and sometimes it's helpful to add a bit of magic to bind their tongues. Cord magic is a popular tool in a number of folk magic traditions. Use this spell if someone is spreading rumors and lies, or just discussing your business. Use a black cord to banish this individual's gossipy ways and tie his or her tongue in knots. Feel free to include the name of the person who is the focus of your spell.

Begin by tying a knot in the cord about 4 inches from one end. Tie eight more knots—for a total of nine—at equal distance apart. Make each knot as tight as you can, and as you tie each one, say *I tie your tongue from harmful words, I tie your tongue from gossip, I tie your tongue from speaking of me.*

Once you've tied all nine knots, take the knotted cord and bury or hide it somewhere near the person's house or property.

January 20

Aquarius
Spell for Compassion

You'll need:
- Your favorite incense
- A feather

In the traditional Zodiac, January 20 is the first day of the sign of Aquarius. Although most people think of this sign as being connected to water, it's actually an Air sign. If you'd like to help yourself be a little more compassionate and patient when dealing with others, this spell is a good place to start.

Light your incense, and watch as the smoke rises into the air. Imagine your own short temper or impatience rising along with it. Think about how easy it is to become intolerant and judgmental toward others, then picture your shortcomings drifting away like the smoke of your incense. Use the feather to fan the smoke, dispersing it out into the universe. As you do so, say *I will be patient, I will be kind, I will be understanding. I will embrace compassion, and send my negative feelings away. I will be fair and just to others, as I would ask them to be toward me in return.*

January 21

Confident Communication Spell

You'll need:
- A tiger's eye stone
- Red string or embroidery floss

M ercury is known as the messenger of the gods, and in some traditions is honored on January 21. His confidence is part of what makes him an effective communicator. Do this spell if you've got a big speech coming up, a presentation in front of a large group, or a pending personal conversation that makes you nervous. If possible, do this spell on a Wednesday, which is associated with Mercury and communication.

Taking your time, wrap the tiger's eye stone in the red floss. Picture yourself trapping your courage inside the stone, binding it tight with the string. As you continue to wrap it, say *I speak with clarity and courage, I speak with confidence and strength, I speak with self-assuredness and authority, I speak with poise and conviction.*

Carry the wrapped stone in your pocket when it's time to speak, and feel the courage within yourself.

January 22

Banish
Your Bad Habit

You'll need:
- Paper and a pen
- Helium-filled black balloons on a string, one
for each habit you want to eliminate

As January progresses, and you work on setting goals and making plans for the rest of the year, it's also important to eliminate the bad habits that might be dragging you down. Is this the year for you to quit smoking or drinking? Eliminate some reckless behavior? Maybe it's time to change your unhealthy eating habits. Whatever you need to get rid of, send it away so you can start anew. Go outside on a breezy, windy day to do this spell.

Write your bad habits on individual pieces of paper. You can keep it simple, writing SMOKING, UNHEALTHY EATING, or DRINKING TOO OFTEN. Roll each piece of paper up in a tube, and tie it to a balloon, using the attached string. Wait for a good strong gust of wind to come along, and then release your balloons—and your bad habits—into the wild! As they float away on the breeze, wave good-bye. Feel free to shout, if you like, saying things like *Don't come back!* or *I'm not going to miss you!* Keep waving until the balloons vanish in the distance.

Try to make this a celebratory event—after all, getting rid of bad habits means you can make plenty of room for new ones.

January 23

The Chill-Out Spell

You'll need:
- A marker
- A bay leaf
- A zip-top plastic bag
- Snow

For a lot of us, January is a month full of snow, ice, and miserably cold weather. Why not use that to your advantage, and get a pest to chill out? Perhaps you have a coworker who harasses you constantly, or a neighbor who lets his dog poop on your lawn. Maybe you have a creepy ex who likes to drive past your house. These are exactly the sorts of people for which this spell is designed. If you can do this outside, it's even better!

Write on the bay leaf the name of the person who has been driving you nuts. Place the bay leaf in the plastic bag, then pack it full of snow. As you do so, say *A time to freeze, a time to chill, a time to back off, and to follow my will.*

Place the bag in your freezer, and leave it there for as long as you need to keep the person away from you.

January 24

The Beer Can Spell

You'll need:
- Metal snippers
- An empty beer can
- A pair (or two) of pliers
- A hammer

On January 24, 1935, the Gottfried Krueger Brewing Company debuted the first canned beer. It was such a big hit with test customers that they immediately ramped up production, and the rest is history. Beer cans are made from aluminum, which is typically associated with deflection of negative energy. Has someone been sending bad vibes your way? Beer cans are incredibly easy to get your hands on, so use one to create a magic mirror–type talisman or amulet.

Use the snippers to cut the top and bottom off the beer can, and then cut open the cylinder to create a single rectangular piece of aluminum. Use the pliers to fold over any sharp edges, and the hammer to pound them flat. Bend the aluminum into any shape you like, with the unprinted shiny side facing outward, using the pliers and hammer so your folds are as tight as possible. As you fold the aluminum inward, focus outward, so any negative energy that comes your way will be reflected back to the sender. Keep your folded aluminum mirror in the place where it will be most effective—your desk at work, an unobtrusive spot in your kitchen, or even in your pocket.

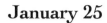

January 25

Burns Night
Love-Sweetening Spell

You'll need:

- Honey
- A jar with a lid
- A red rose

Robert Burns, a well-known Scottish poet, was quite a romantic. His life is honored annually on January 25, with celebrations involving a haggis, a goodly amount of alcohol, and poetry recitals. You don't need a haggis to do this spell, which is designed to sweeten a love relationship. Instead, use flower petals, in honor of Burns's famous poem, "My Love is Like a Red, Red Rose." Try to do this spell on a Friday, which is associated with love.

Pour the honey into the jar. Slowly pluck the petals off the rose, and add them to the honey one by one. As you do, say *Our love is sweet, our love is passionate, our love is alive. With care and compassion, our love will thrive.*

Once you've placed all the rose petals in the honey, put the lid on the jar and seal it tightly. Hide the jar somewhere in your home; under the bed is an ideal location.

January 26

Star Magic
Wish Spell

You'll need:
- A white candle
- A piece of paper and a pen

Do you remember wishing upon a star when you were a child? In January, the nights are cold and clear, and often we can see the stars shining brightly above us. This is a good month to make wishes that involve self-improvement and transformation. Go outside at sunset and keep your eyes on the skies for the first star to appear.

Light the candle as you watch the sun set. Take the time to think about your goal. What do you wish to achieve this year? Financial success? Furthering your education? Perhaps you just want to be a better person overall. Write your wish on the paper, and fold it three times. When you see the first star in the sky, hold the paper up in the air, and say *Star above, shining bright, I wish upon you this cool, clear night. I'll make big changes, as I need to, and make all this year's wishes come true.*

Think about what you're going to do to make your dreams come true this year, and then blow out the candle. Place the folded paper under your pillow and keep it there as you sleep for the next nine nights.

January 27

Rose Quartz
Healing Blessings

You'll need:
• Three blue candles • A rose quartz stone

As you wrap up the month of January, it's not a bad idea to think about your health in the coming year. While there are many gemstones and crystals associated with specific types of healing magic, you can use a rose quartz as a sort of all-purpose healing crystal. Do this spell for healing blessings for yourself or those you love; use one stone for each of the people to whom you are sending healing blessings. If possible, do this spell on a Sunday, which is associated with health and the spirit.

Light the candles in a triangle formation, and place the rose quartz in the center. Cover the stone with your hands and close your eyes. Imagine healing blessings coming from the universe and spreading throughout your body, starting with the palms and fingers, up your arms, and working through down to your toes, and up to the top of your head. If your working includes other people, imagine that healing energy spreading from your body to theirs, so you and your loved ones are enveloped in physical and mental wellness.

As you focus on this spread of energy, say *Healing magic, peace and calm, I am healthy, mentally, physically, and spiritually. I will be healthy all year, in my mind, body, and soul.*

When you have finished, extinguish the candles. Keep the rose quartz in your pocket, and hold it periodically to help recharge your healing energy.

January 28

Garlic Salt
Protection Spell

You'll need:
- Sea salt
- Garlic power

Garlic can be used as a deterrent to keep troublesome people out of your home. Salt has been used in many magical traditions to delineate sacred space. Combine the two to make a magical boundary around your home.

Combine equal parts sea salt and garlic powder in a bowl or a bag. Mix them together until they're well blended. Go outside and, starting at your front door, walk slowly around your home in a clockwise direction. As you walk, sprinkle the garlic salt blend on the ground, and say *My home is safe, my home is sacred, my home is protected. None shall enter who would do me harm.*

Keep a mixture of salt and garlic powder on hand, and periodically replenish it around the perimeter of your home, paying extra attention to doors and windows.

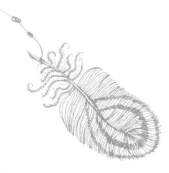

January 29

Baseball Spell to
Get Rid of Your Fears

You'll need:

- A red marker
- A baseball or a softball
- A ball bat

On January 29, 1936, the Baseball Hall of Fame elected its first members in Cooperstown, New York, including Babe Ruth. If you've ever wondered about using nonmagical items in spellwork, this is a perfect example of what you can do when you think outside the box. Babe Ruth was famous for many things, but the iconic image of him calling his shot to center field in the 1932 World Series is known the world over. You can use a similar method to banish fears that may be holding you back. If you don't have access to a baseball stadium, find a large empty field in which to do this. Use a red marker for courage.

Figure out which fears are limiting your success, and write them on the ball. Point off in the distance toward the horizon, calling your shot. This is the direction in which you're going to send those fears. Hold the bat, toss the ball straight up in the air, and take a swing. Whack it as hard as you can! If it doesn't travel too far, don't worry. Walk to where the ball is sitting, pick it up, and take another swing. Keep going until you've sent the ball, and your fears, as far from your starting point as you can.

January 30

Cold Moon
Intuition Magic

You'll need:
- A bowl of water
- A silver candle

Ever have a gut feeling about something? That's your intuition talking to you. January is often the time of the Cold Moon, which is associated with wisdom and intuition. This simple moon working will help you get in touch with your intuitive side, and help you learn to trust your instinct. Do this spell outside on the night of the full moon, or one of the three nights prior to it. Magical bonus points if you can do this spell on a Monday, which is associated with moon energy and intuition!

Place the bowl on a flat surface, positioned so the moon is reflected in the water. Focus on the reflection, and allow yourself to stop worrying about mundane things. As you clear your mind of the nonmagical, you may notice that you're beginning to see images, patterns, and shapes reflected in the water. You may even want to note what you see so you can go back to it later. Let yourself interpret these things in any direction your mind takes you, even if it doesn't make sense initially. This is your intuition working.

Once you begin to feel restless or bored, stop trying to see new things. Pour the water out in your garden or yard, and offer a quick thanks to the moon for helping you see with clarity.

January 31

Valkyrie Spell for Strength and Fortitude

You'll need:
- Allspice
- Powdered ginger
- Pure vanilla extract

In Norse legend, the Valkyries were a host of shieldmaidens who guided fallen warriors to the hall of Odin. They were known for being brave and strong. Some modern Norse traditions observe their day on January 31. Take advantage of this resilient feminine energy to do a spell for inner strength and bravery, using three kitchen items that are associated with courage and fortitude.

Blend the allspice and ginger together, then add a teaspoon or two of the vanilla extract. Mix some more, and as you do so, say *I am brave and strong, I am courageous and bold, I am fearless and daring, I am valiant and honorable, I am relentless and unstoppable.*

Anoint yourself with the vanilla blend behind your ears and on your wrists before stepping into a new challenge.

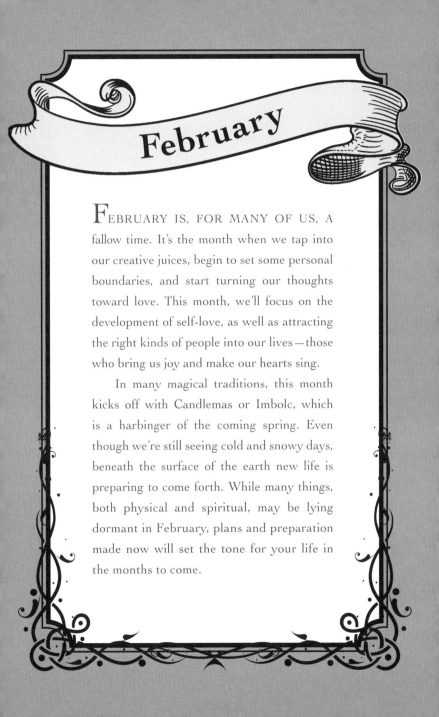

February

FEBRUARY IS, FOR MANY OF US, A fallow time. It's the month when we tap into our creative juices, begin to set some personal boundaries, and start turning our thoughts toward love. This month, we'll focus on the development of self-love, as well as attracting the right kinds of people into our lives—those who bring us joy and make our hearts sing.

In many magical traditions, this month kicks off with Candlemas or Imbolc, which is a harbinger of the coming spring. Even though we're still seeing cold and snowy days, beneath the surface of the earth new life is preparing to come forth. While many things, both physical and spiritual, may be lying dormant in February, plans and preparation made now will set the tone for your life in the months to come.

February 1

Imbolc Offerings to the Land

You'll need:
- Milk
- An egg

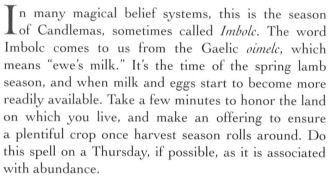

In many magical belief systems, this is the season of Candlemas, sometimes called *Imbolc*. The word Imbolc comes to us from the Gaelic *oimelc*, which means "ewe's milk." It's the time of the spring lamb season, and when milk and eggs start to become more readily available. Take a few minutes to honor the land on which you live, and make an offering to ensure a plentiful crop once harvest season rolls around. Do this spell on a Thursday, if possible, as it is associated with abundance.

Pour the milk into a bowl, and crack the egg into it. Beat the egg until you have a frothy blend. Walk the perimeter of your garden, and use your fingers to splash the milk-and-egg mixture on the ground, a few droplets at a time. As you do, say *Winter draws to an end, and spring grows near. New life will be coming soon. I honor the land with a simple offering, and ask for abundance and plenty in exchange.* Continue circling your garden until the bowl is empty.

If you don't have a garden in your yard, splash the mixture into your potted plants.

February 2

Groundhog Day
Do-Over Spell

You'll need:
- A piece of paper and a pen
- A basil leaf
- A yellow ribbon

In American folklore, Groundhog Day is typically a time when we watch the news to see if a large rodent can predict the end of winter. However, thanks to Hollywood, February 2 has also become symbolic of repetition and second chances. If you've made some mistakes recently, this is a good day to give yourself a shot at redemption. Treat yourself to the luxury of a do-over. If your errors from the past involve the way you've acted toward another person, be sure to let this individual know you're ready to make amends. You'll use a basil leaf, which is associated with mending quarrels, and a yellow ribbon for persuasion.

Write a letter to the person you've wronged—if your mistakes affect no one but you, address the letter to yourself. Go into detail about what you've done, and how you would do things differently if you had another chance. When you're done, sign the letter and fold it three times, with the basil leaf tucked inside. Tie it shut with the yellow ribbon, and sleep with it tucked under your pillow for nine nights in a row. After the ninth night, burn the letter in your fireplace or in a fireproof bowl, and say *Good-bye*. Be sure to recognize your opportunities for do-overs when they present themselves.

February 3

Setsubun-sai
Spell to Drive Out
Misfortune

You'll need:
- Uncooked soybeans
- A pan
- A bowl

In Japan, February 3 is the day of the ancient Shinto festival called Setsubun-sai. One of the most important aspects of this celebration, which honors the end of winter, is the *mame-maki* tradition. Mame-maki is a ritual designed to drive out the seeds of misfortune. Soybeans are roasted in advance, which ensures new misfortunes can't germinate and grow during the coming year.

Soak the soybeans overnight in water, then drain them. Roast them in a pan on your stovetop over low heat. Once the soybeans have roasted, allow them to cool on a paper towel, and place them in a bowl. Open each door and window in your home, and toss a few soybeans outside. As you do so, say *Ill fortune out, bad luck out, old things out! Good fortune in, good luck in, new things in!*

In some celebrations, after the roasted beans are cast out, each family member eats one bean for every year in their age. If you decide to do this, make sure you roast enough beans!

February 4

King Frost
Snow Spell for
Neighborhood Harmony

You'll need:
- Sticks, carrots, hats, and scarves
- Snow

In London, February 4 was celebrated as King Frost Day from the fifteenth to the nineteenth centuries. During these four hundred or so years, the River Thames often froze over so completely that people could walk from one side to the other. Many of us are now surrounded by snow, so why not take advantage of it and use snow to create harmony with your neighbors?

Use the snow to create snowmen around your yard, facing each of your neighbors' homes. As you build them, say *Friends and neighbors, neighbors and friends, harmony and community that never ends.* Adorn your snowmen with carrot noses, scarves, and hats, with the sticks for arms—feel free to position them in a jaunty wave to the neighbors!

February 5

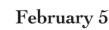

Wyrd Sisters Divination

You'll need:
- A silver candle
- A mirror

There's an Old English word, *wyrd*, that means fate or prophecy. It's often associated with the Wyrd Sisters, or the Three Fates, in classical mythology. In some magical traditions, wyrd is used in terms of divination—you can take advantage of this, and do a little foresight of your own to see what the future may hold. Do this spell at night, in a dark room.

Light the candle so it provides the only source of illumination in the room, and place it behind you. Look in the mirror and allow your mind to wander. If there's a specific question to which you need the answer, focus on this issue as you gaze into the mirror. Say *Reveal to me what I must know, uncover for me what lies ahead, show me what I must change.*

Watch for images and shapes to appear in the mirror, reflected in the flickering candlelight. You may even wish to write things down so you can evaluate them later. If you see visions of what you need to do differently to change the potential outcome of your situation, start making those adjustments the next morning.

February 6

Checkbook
Abundance Spell

You'll need:
• A blank check

L et's face it: We all need and want things to which we don't have immediate access. Sometimes we can attain those goals with a bit of extra cash. If you're hoping to achieve a little more financial flexibility, try doing this abundance spell to bring more money your way—you may be surprised how it manifests! Try to do this working on a Thursday, which is associated with money and abundance.

Make out the check to yourself, with this year's date on it. Don't include a specific dollar amount, but simply write ENOUGH in the space where you would normally write a number, then sign it at the bottom. As you write out your check, say *A blank check to make prosperity flow, to make money multiply and fortune grow.*

Take a moment to think about what you will do with any extra cash. Will you use it to go back to school? Pay off a bill? Buy some extra groceries? Place the check in a safe place where it can remain undisturbed and out of sight.

February 7

Snowdrop Blessing to Welcome Spring

You'll need:
- A white candle
- Snowdrop blossoms

Snowdrops are some of the first spring flowers we see each year. They're called snowdrops because they often begin to bloom before the last of the snow has even melted. Depending on where you live, you may see them as early as February, despite the chilly temperatures. This flower is associated with hope, peace, and purification. If you're lucky enough to see snowdrops, do this simple blessing to welcome the coming spring. Do this spell outside, first thing in the morning, as the sun rises.

Light the candle, and hold the snowdrop blossoms in your hands. Say *Harmony and hope, unity and love, light in the dark, and peace to all. As winter ends and spring draws near, may we all rejoice in the return of new life.*

Leave the candle outside to burn out on its own, and scatter the snowdrop blossoms around your front door.

February 8

Feng Shui
Good Luck Spell

You'll need:
- A piece of red ribbon or yarn
- Nine Chinese coins

The date of the Chinese New Year celebration varies, but it typically falls in January or February. In Feng Shui, which is a Chinese philosophy that embraces harmony with our surroundings, red is associated with good luck, and coins are often used as tokens of good fortune. Do this working with a red ribbon and the Chinese coins that have a hole in the center.

Thread the coins on the ribbon so they are all facing in the same direction. As you do so, count them off, saying *One coin for luck, two coins for prosperity, three coins for abundance, four coins for fortune, five coins for happiness, six coins for love, seven coins for blessings, eight coins for joy, nine coins for all good things that life has to offer.* Knot the ribbon, and either wear the coins around your wrist as a bracelet, carry them in your pocket, or hang them in a spot in your home where you can see them every day.

February 9

Healing Spell
for the Winter Blues

You'll need:
- Three blue candles
- Thyme, fresh or dried

February 9 is the feast day of the sun god Apollo, who is associated with healing, among his many other attributes. By this point in the year, many of us are feeling off-kilter mentally and spiritually because of the long, dark nights and the chilly winter temperatures that keep us indoors. Do this healing spell to give yourself a bit of a spiritual boost from the winter blues.

Light the three candles one at a time. As you light each, say *Heal my mind, my spirit, my soul, I shall be healthy and happy and whole.* Once the candles are lit, hold the thyme* leaves between your palms, and slowly rub them together, saying *Winter will end, the sun returns once more, my spirits will rise, and my soul will soar.*

Extinguish the candles, and scatter the crushed thyme leaves outside.

*A few people are sensitive to the oils in thyme leaves.
If you can't tolerate thyme, use another herb associated with healing,
such as chamomile or honeysuckle.*

February 10

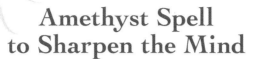

Amethyst Spell
to Sharpen the Mind

You'll need:
• An amethyst stone

A methyst is the birthstone associated with February, and it's also connected to wisdom and learning. Specifically, it's a good stone to use in spells that help you gain a bit of mental clarity. If you're having trouble focusing on tasks at work or school, an amethyst spell can give your brain a bit of a lift.

Lie down in a comfortable spot where you can be undisturbed for a few moments. Hold the amethyst in your hands and think about the sort of help you need. Do you need to boost your time-management skills? Develop better work or study habits? Focus on the specific aspects of your thought process that you need to jump-start. After a few minutes, you may notice that the amethyst is beginning to feel warm. Place it under your pillow so your brain will benefit from its magical properties while you sleep.

February 11

Playing Card Love Divination

You'll need:
• A standard deck
of 52 playing cards

In February, many of us turn our focus to matters of the heart. If you have your eye on someone and you're not sure if he or she returns your feelings, do a bit of love divination to figure out where you really stand.

Shuffle the cards as you think about the person in whom you're interested. Once you've gotten them good and mixed up, randomly draw thirteen cards from the deck. Turn them over to see what they say:

MOSTLY HEARTS—the person returns your feelings, although he or she may not have made this known to you.

MOSTLY CLUBS—there are obstacles in the way that must be overcome before you can have a relationship.

MOSTLY DIAMONDS—the person may be interested in you, but he or she has other interests that take priority.

MOSTLY SPADES—he or she doesn't feel the same way you do.

February 12

Lover's
Cookie Spell

You'll need:
• Your favorite cookie recipe and ingredients
• A pastry brush
• Melted butter

Few things in this world are appreciated as much as home-baked cookies. If you've fallen for someone, and you want to make this person aware of your feelings but aren't quite ready to formally declare your love, start by baking a batch of delicious treats.

Bake the cookies according to the recipe. After they've come out of the oven, dip the pastry brush in the melted butter, and paint a heart on each cookie. Don't worry—as they cool, the butter will be absorbed and the hearts won't be visible. As you paint the hearts, say *Words can't express what it's hard to say, so these cookies bring my message of love your way.*

Give the person a gift of cookies—they're even better if you serve them still warm!

February 13

Ancestor Spell to Strengthen Family Ties

You'll need:
- Photos of your ancestors
- A glass of milk or another beverage
- Bread, preferably homemade

We may love our family members, but they can be a challenge to handle. In ancient Rome, February 13 was the celebration of the Parentalia festival, in which the ancestors were honored and called upon as a demonstration of family strength and loyalty. This is a good time to invoke your own ancestors to help build the ties and bonds of kinship. Do this working at sunset.

Arrange the photos so you can see all of your ancestors' faces. Raise the glass of milk to them in a toast, and say *Clan and kin, blood and bone, I am honored that you are all part of who I am.* Take a drink of the milk. Raise the bread to your ancestors, and say *Hearth and home, family and fealty, may we all be faithful to one another.* Take a bite of the bread.

Finally, say *Our family is strong, our ties are unbreakable, our loyalty never wavers, our love knows no boundaries.* Spend a few moments reflecting on the traits you've inherited from the people in your bloodline, and know that their strength runs through you. Leave out the bread and milk as an offering to your ancestors overnight, and dispose of it in the morning.

February 14

Valentine's Spell
to Love Yourself

You'll need:
• A bag of candy message hearts
• A mirror

Many magical traditions have injunctions against doing love spells on other people—but that's okay, because sometimes we need to focus on loving ourselves. Once we learn to do that, other people find us a lot easier to love in return. Often we're far more willing to show other people love than we are ourselves. That's why we're going to let those little candy hearts with messages do the talking for us!

Open the bag of candy hearts and pour them into a bowl. Close your eyes and pick a candy at random. Open your eyes, look into the mirror, and read yourself the message on the heart. Does it say YOU'RE AWESOME or HOT STUFF or KISS ME on it? Repeat the message to yourself in the mirror three times, and say it like you mean it! After you've done this, eat the candy heart—and then do it again, until you've read yourself nine different messages and eaten the candies. Spend the rest of the day thinking about how fantastic you are, and how you're worthy of love from other people.

February 15

Angry Snow

You'll need:
- A bucket
- Snow

Sometimes we get angry for no reason—or, worse yet, we have reasons, but we express our feelings inappropriately. Instead of taking out your rage and frustration on those around you, why not channel it someplace innocuous, and get rid of it in a way that won't upset anyone else? Make a bucket of Angry Snow! Do this spell on the morning after a snowstorm.

Fill the bucket with freshly fallen snow. Imagine all the things that make you frustrated and angry right now, and picture those things traveling from your brain into your hands. Once your anger is revved up and centered in your fingertips, plunge your hands into the bucket of snow. As you do, say *Anger be gone, into the snow, away from me, into the snow, out of my heart, into the snow, out of my mind, and into the snow.*

Pull your hands out of the bucket—you don't want to get frostbite! Take the bucket someplace far from your home, and dump the snow on the ground. As the snow gradually melts away, so will your anger.

February 16

Lipstick Spell to Eliminate Sibling Rivalry

You'll need:
- A photo of your sibling
- Your favorite lipstick

Most of us love our siblings, but there are times when they drive us nuts. Especially as adults, sibling rivalry can create quite a rift in the relationship. No matter which of you is at fault, you can do this spell to remove sibling rivalry.

Put on your lipstick—if you don't normally wear it, use moisturizing lip balm instead. Hold the photo of your sibling in your dominant hand, and say *Family ties, a bond of the heart, jealousy will never tear us apart. Rivals no more, we're siblings and friends, envy is gone, the conflict now ends.*

Kiss the photo of your sibling, leaving a lipstick mark on the cheek. Tuck it in your purse or wallet, and carry it with you next time you interact with your brother or sister.

February 17

Oven Spell
for Home Blessings

You'll need:
- A clean oven
- Your favorite bread recipe and ingredients

February 17 was the day of the Fornacalia festival, a celebration of the goddess Fornax. A patron deity of ovens, she is associated with baking bread and cakes to be used in sacred rituals. This is a good day to do a thorough cleaning of your kitchen, especially the oven, and then wrap things up with a household blessing for family harmony.

Prepare the bread according to the recipe. As you're kneading the dough, visualize a harmonious and stable home, saying *Bread for the hearth, bread for the home, bread for this house, bread for this family.* Once the bread is prepared, place it in the clean oven to bake.

After you take it out of the oven and let it cool, cut it into slices. As you do, say *Hospitality for all, health for all, happiness for all, and harmony for all.* Include the freshly baked bread as part of your family dinner so everyone can enjoy the magic.

February 18

Spell to
Stop a Liar

You'll need:
- A pen
- A bay leaf
- A package of ground meat

We've all encountered liars in our lives. Sometimes they're family members, coworkers, or those we thought were our friends. People lie for a variety of reasons, but one common thread is that untruthful speech, no matter its motivation, can be hurtful and damaging. If someone is spreading lies about you or a person you love, use this simple spell to stop it. Use a bay leaf, associated with communication, for this working.

Write the name of the liar on the bay leaf and tear it into the smallest possible pieces. As you do so, say *No more lies from you, no more falsehood, no more untruth.* Mix the shredded bay leaf into the ground meat, and using your hands, form the meat into a log shaped like a human tongue. As you're shaping the meat, say *Your tongue is silent, your words are unheard, your voice speaks ill of me no more.*

Leave the meat tongue on the ground somewhere near the liar's property. Be mindful of outdoor pets when you do this!

February 19

Pisces Spell for Forgiveness

You'll need:
- A pink candle
- A rose—if possible, one that was given to you by the person you hurt
- A jar of water with a lid

In astrology, the Zodiac sign of Pisces kicks in on February 19. A water sign, Pisces is often associated with empathy and emotional understanding. If you've noticed that your emotions are causing you to say things that are hurtful to others, this is a good day to remedy this practice with a simple working. Try to do this on a Friday, which is often associated with reconciliation.

Light the candle, and hold the rose in your hand. Consider the words you said that were unkind, thoughtless, or cruel. As you reflect on them, slowly remove the petals from the rose, one at a time. Set them alight in the candle's flame, and drop them into the jar of water as they burn, saying *Forgive my words, forgive my actions, forgive my mistakes.*

After all the rose petals are in the jar, put the lid on it and bury it in your yard. Make sure you show the person you hurt that he or she can trust you once more.

February 20

Patchouli Love Sachet

You'll need:
- Dried patchouli
- A rose quartz stone
- A small cloth bag with a drawstring

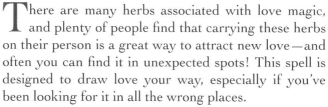

There are many herbs associated with love magic, and plenty of people find that carrying these herbs on their person is a great way to attract new love—and often you can find it in unexpected spots! This spell is designed to draw love your way, especially if you've been looking for it in all the wrong places.

Place the patchouli and rose quartz in the cloth bag, and pull the drawstring tight. Hold the bag close to your heart, and say *I am worthy of love, I am deserving of love, I am ready to love, and be loved in return. Love will come to me, love will find me, love is out there for me, and it will appear to me.*

Keep the sachet in your pocket when you're out and about—you might be surprised at who you encounter, and how they feel about you!

February 21

Teddy Bear
Dream Spell for Children

You'll need:

- A blue ribbon
- A bundle of lavender
- A teddy bear

On February 21, 1903, the teddy bear made its commercial debut. Named for President Theodore "Teddy" Roosevelt, the cuddly creature was an instant success with parents and children alike. More than a century later, most kids have a teddy bear, and the toy can come in handy as a protector. If you have a child who's been struggling with unpleasant dreams, or if you have experienced restless sleep, use a bit of teddy bear magic. Do this spell at night, right before bedtime.

Use the ribbon to tie the lavender around the teddy bear's neck. As you do so, say *Power in this teddy bear, he chases bad dreams out of there, teddy bear magic as we sleep, good dreams in the night he'll keep.* If your child is old enough, have him or her say it along with you, then tuck the teddy bear into bed with your young one for the night.

February 22

Spell to Set Boundaries

You'll need:
- A box of large iron nails
- A hammer or mallet

The Terminalia festival fell on February 22, and was a time for landowners to mark the boundaries of their holdings. Today we have official property lines to set legal and civil boundaries, but sometimes that doesn't prevent people from trespassing. Use this spell to set a metaphysical barrier around the perimeter of your property. The ground may still be frozen or covered in snow, so keep a large hammer or mallet handy.

Walk the perimeter of your property in a clockwise direction. Stop at regular intervals, and pound an iron nail—or even railroad spikes, if you can find them—into the ground with the hammer. As you do so, say loudly, *This land is mine, this property is mine. Let none enter that would do us harm. This land is my home, this property is my home, and it is sacred and safe.*

Periodically refresh the boundary by adding more nails to give the spell a little boost.

February 23

Prosperity Seeds

You'll need:
- Small pots
- Potting soil and water
- Seeds for plants such as chamomile, basil, pennyroyal, and clover

Even though it's not quite the right time of year to put seeds into the ground—at least in most areas—you can still get a jump on your spring planting. Gardening is a magical act, so why not sow the seeds of prosperity while you're planning your garden for the coming year? Use seeds that will bring you blossoms associated with prosperity magic. Do this spell on a sunny day.

Fill each of the pots with the appropriate amount of potting soil. Place the seeds in the pots, following the directions on the packaging. As you push them into the soil, say *Cool dark earth blessed with abundance, tiny seeds blessed with life, bright warm sun blessed with power. May these plants be blessed as the earth becomes fruitful, bringing forth prosperity to my life.*

Add water to the soil, and place the pots in a sunny window so they can begin to germinate. When the danger of frost has passed, plant them in your garden.

February 24

Spell to
Nail a Job Interview

You'll need:
• Two green candles

Do you have a job interview coming up? Good for you! In addition to all the mundane things you'll need to do to prepare, like dressing for success and rehearsing answers to common interview questions, it never hurts to give yourself a little magical boost. Begin doing this spell three days prior to the interview—but if it's less than three days away, don't worry, you can still do it!

Procure a business card from the person with whom you're interviewing.* Light the candles, and start thinking about all the things you have to offer the company. Place the business card between the candles, and begin speaking to it as though you were talking to the interviewer. What is your skill set? Can you detail your experience and accomplishments? It's time to sell yourself to that business card, and explain why you're the best person for this new position. Once you've done this to your satisfaction, extinguish the candles, but leave the business card in a place where you can see it. Every time you walk past it for the next three days, greet it professionally, and remind it why you should be the company's newest employee.

If you don't have access to the person's business card, cut out a piece of paper the size of a business card, and write the interviewer's name, company, and contact information on it.

February 25

Battery Spell to Jump-Start Your Love Life

You'll need:
- A pair of batteries the same size
- A piece of red fabric

If you've been in a relationship any length of time, you know that sometimes the blazing fires of passion dwindle to a tiny flame. As long as that spark is still there, small as it may be, it's worth rekindling! Give your love life a jump-start to kick the passion back into overdrive.

Wrap the batteries, touching each other, tightly in the red fabric. As you do, say *With time, passion may sometimes fade, but our love still burns. We will rekindle the spark, rejoice in our love, and return to the fire we felt before. The power, passion, and energy of love is ours to claim.*

Place the fabric-wrapped batteries under your bed so they'll be close to you and your lover.

February 26

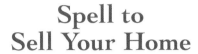

Spell to
Sell Your Home

You'll need:
- A sage smudge stick
- Grape-seed oil
- Your realtor's For Sale yard sign

In many areas, the real estate market picks up in the spring. If you're selling your house, late February is a good time to do this working because it will give you an advantage as those spring house-hunters come through your home. Be sure to give your house a thorough physical cleaning, from top to bottom, before doing this spell. Try to do this first thing in the morning, as the sun rises.

Light the sage, and walk the inside perimeter of your house, starting at the north side. Pass the sage along the walls, doors, and windows. As you do this, say out loud all the things that are great about the house and would make it appealing to a buyer. Narrate the features you would like a realtor to highlight, such as, *Here, we have lovely French doors leading out to a private deck,* or *The kitchen was remodeled just two years ago, with brand-new stainless steel appliances.* Do this through the entire house.

When you've finished inside, go to the front yard. Dip your finger in the oil, and use it to draw a dollar sign on each side of the For Sale sign. As you do so, talk to potential buyers. You don't know who they are, but you know they want that house, so tell them. *You will LOVE this place! The area is quiet, great schools, nice neighbors,* and so on. When you are done, sprinkle the remainder of the oil mixture around the outside perimeter of the house.

February 27

Quickening Moon
Spell for Self-Esteem

You'll need:

• Seven pieces of paper and a pen

In February, the full moon is called the Quickening Moon. It's the time of year when the earth itself is quickening, as seeds deep in the earth begin their journey toward the light. On a metaphysical level, it's a time for reinvention and renewal. If you've been feeling less than positive about yourself, do this spell on the night of the full moon, as well as the three nights before and the three nights after, to give your self-esteem a pick-me-up.

On the first night, begin by writing on one of the pieces of paper something you love about yourself. Include things like *I love my crazy sense of humor* or *I love my free-spirited style*. Each night, write another affirmation, and take a moment to reread the ones you've already written. Tuck them under your pillow when you go to bed. By the final night, you'll have seven things you love about yourself. Carry them in your purse or your pocket, and pull them out when you need a reminder of how great you are.

February 28

Dream
Lover Spell

You'll need:
- Rosemary, either fresh or dried
- A photo of your potential lover
- Mugwort

Many magical traditions believe that if you dream about someone, he or she may be dreaming of you at the same time. If you've been fantasizing about someone during your waking hours and you're not sure this person is into you, try meeting up with him or her in your dreams. You'll be using rosemary, which is associated with dreams, and mugwort, which is believed to encourage astral travel. Do this spell right before you fall asleep.

Place the rosemary and mugwort under your pillow. Lie in bed, holding the photo. Relax and let your breathing become steady, and as you gaze at the photo of your potential lover, say *Dream of me as I dream of you, meeting in the night. Share your dreams and I'll share mine, until the morning light.* Repeat this until you doze off.

February 29

Birthday
Good Luck Spell

You'll need:
- A cupcake with a candle in your favorite color
- A shiny new penny

Thanks to the Leap Year situation, we see February 29 only once every four years. Think of this spell as a magical bonus round that you can use to celebrate your birthday, whenever it may happen to fall. It's your magical day, so why not give yourself the gift of an entire year of good luck?

Place the cupcake in front of you and light the candle. If you want to sing the Happy Birthday song to yourself, go right ahead. Hold the penny in your hands tightly, and think about the things that define good luck. Focus all your good luck thoughts on the penny, and say *It's my birthday, I'm one year older, one year wiser, and one year bolder. A year of fortune comes my way, to celebrate my special day.*

As you think about your pending good luck, blow out the candle. Keep the penny in your pocket or your wallet for the rest of the year.

March

THE MONTH OF MARCH IS NAMED for the warrior god Mars. It's a time of stormy energy and wild weather, and we begin to see new life returning as the spring season arrives. This month we'll focus on rebirth and renewal, as well as strength and the ability to conquer our challenges.

For some modern magical traditions, this is the sason of Ostara, the spring equinox. It's a time of balance, with equal hours of light and darkness. This is a good month to plant seeds—both physical and spiritual—so later in the year your life will be full of abundance.

March 1

Pomander Spell
for a Balanced Partnership

You'll need:
- A pink ribbon
- A large orange
- Whole cloves

March 1 is the day of the festival of Juno Luciana, a goddess of marital harmony. One of the biggest challenges any married couple faces is maintaining balance in the relationship. If a marriage is a partnership, you may have to put some work into making things equal. Try to do this spell on a Friday, which is connected to love magic.

Wrap the pink ribbon around the orange so it is divided into two equal halves. Be sure to leave a loop at the top. Press the cloves into the skin of the orange, going from one side to the other in equal numbers. As you do, say *Two halves of a whole, we are one. Our marriage is fair, our marriage is equal. We are partners in life and in love.*

Continue adding cloves to the orange, making sure there is the same number on each half. Once you are done, hang your orange pomander in your kitchen or bedroom.

March 2

Sacred Spring
Spell for Cleansing

You'll need:
- Sea salt
- A jar with a lid
- A source of moving water

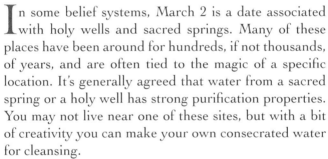

In some belief systems, March 2 is a date associated with holy wells and sacred springs. Many of these places have been around for hundreds, if not thousands, of years, and are often tied to the magic of a specific location. It's generally agreed that water from a sacred spring or a holy well has strong purification properties. You may not live near one of these sites, but with a bit of creativity you can make your own consecrated water for cleansing.

Place the sea salt in the jar, and leave it outside in the sun for three days. On the final day, take the jar to your water source—this can be a pond, lake, stream, or even the ocean—and fill it up. Cap it tightly, and when you get home, sprinkle the water around your doors and windows. As you do, say *Sacred water, cleansing and purifying, wash away ills and danger, and bless this home and all who dwell within.*

March 3

Sea Magic Spell
to Find New Friendships

You'll need:
- Nine seashells
- An orange candle

In mythology, Aegir is a mythical being associated with the sea, known for elaborate parties he hosts for the gods. March 3 is his festival day, so today is a good time to do a bit of socializing, and cultivate friendships with people you know only peripherally. The orange candle represents attraction that is not necessarily romantic. This spell comes in especially handy if you have just moved to a new place or started a new job.

Place the seashells in a large circle, put the candle in the center, and light it. Working in a clockwise direction, gradually move the seashells a little closer to the candle. As you do so, say *My circle of friends grows ever closer, those I can trust and rely on, and who can trust and rely on me in turn. My circle of friends grows ever stronger, no conditions or demands, just the bonds of love.*

After you've moved the entire circle of seashells three times, extinguish the candle. Leave it in place, along with the candle, for three days and nights.

72

March 4

Aquamarine Spell for a Safe Voyage

You'll need:
- An aquamarine stone
- A yellow ribbon

March's birthstone is aquamarine (although in some traditions it's bloodstone), which is historically associated with sailors, who carried it to guarantee a safe return from their ocean voyages. You can use aquamarine to protect yourself—or someone you love—on journeys, whether you're traveling by car, by plane, or over the water.

Slowly wrap the aquamarine in the yellow ribbon, and while you do, visualize yourself departing from home and arriving safely at your destination. As you wrap it, say *Blessed journeys, safe and sound, blessed travels, safe and sound, blessed adventures, safe and sound.*

Carry the wrapped stone in your pocket as you travel, or pack it in your luggage.

March 5

Spell to Get
the Home You Want

You'll need:
- A photo of the house you want
- Dirt or grass from the new property
- An envelope with a stamp

Are you house hunting? There are a lot of new homes on the market at any given time, and plenty of people are going to fall in love with the same place you did. What can you do to make sure your offer is the one that gets accepted? Magic, of course! Do this spell as soon as you've decided on the house you want—in fact, do it even before your realtor gets around to making the offer on your behalf. If possible, try to time this working so it happens on a Saturday, which is associated with the security and stability of home life.

Hold the photo in your dominant hand, close to your heart, and say *I have chosen you, I will take care of you, I will love you, and you will be my home.* Place the photo, along with the grass or dirt, in the envelope, and seal it, while saying *You are my home, and I claim you as my own.* Address the envelope to yourself, then go to the post office nearest the home you've fallen in love with and mail it. When your envelope arrives, don't open it until the seller has accepted your offer to buy. After you move into the new place, bury the envelope in the yard.

March 6

Spell to Protect
Your Car
from Thieves

You'll need:
• A piece of paper and a pen
• Your car key

If you're concerned about thieves or vandals targeting your car, this simple spell will work to protect your vehicle. You can also use it on motorcycles, campers, or any other form of transportation that has wheels.

Dirt or gravel from the front tire of the vehicle

Trace an outline of your car key on the paper. As you do, say *This car is mine, and none shall touch it. This car is mine, and none shall enter it without my leave. This car is mine, and it is protected*. Sprinkle the dirt on top of the drawing, and fold up the paper securely so no dirt can fall out. Keep the folded paper in the car's glove compartment.

March 7

Forsythia Spell to Draw New Love

You'll need:
- A knife or a toothpick
- A pink candle
- A vase of water
- Stalks of forsythia with unopened buds

By March, you may have begun to notice buds on the forsythia plants. This early spring flower typically blossoms several weeks before winter truly ends, and it is associated with anticipation. If you're feeling a bit restless about the state of your love life as spring rolls in, do this simple spell to draw new love your way as the seasons change.

Use the knife or toothpick to inscribe a heart in the candle, then light it, visualizing the sort of lover you'd like to draw into your life. As you arrange the forsythia stalks in the vase, say *Love to blossom, love to bloom, love to grow, love come soon.* Blow out the candle, but place it next to the vase in a sunny window. As the forsythia buds begin to bloom, new love will start to blossom in your life.

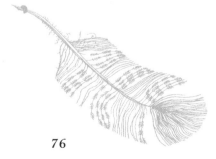

March 8

Rain Boot Spell
to Wash Away Troubles

You'll need:

- A pair of rain boots

There's something infinitely cleansing about a good rainstorm, and March is full of wet weather. It's time for a bit of magical spring cleaning, not only of your home but also your soul and spirit. Wait for a stormy, soggy day, put on your rain boots, and do this spell to wash away your troubles as the new season arrives. If your rain boots are white, even better, as it's associated with purity and cleansing.

Put on your boots and go outside during a rain shower — the wetter, the better. Find the largest puddle on your property, and jump in it. Don't be afraid to splash! Jump up and down in the water, and as you do, say *Troubles wash off when the skies are gray, when the sun returns, they'll go away.*

As you jump, imagine your troubles and dilemmas rolling off your boots and being washed into the puddle. When you're done, take off your boots before entering your home, and leave them outside to dry. As they do, and the puddle evaporates, your troubles will diminish as well.

March 9

Spring Rebirth Bath Sachet

You'll need:
- Rose petals
- Lavender
- A cloth drawstring bag

Spring is a time of renewal and rebirth, when life begins to make its appearance once more. If you've ever thought about reinventing yourself—and the way people see you—March is a good time for this sort of spell. This is a great way not only to give your self-confidence a little boost, but also to magically help you present yourself in a way that others find more attractive.

Combine the rose petals and the lavender in the cloth bag and pull the drawstring tight. Hang the bag over the faucet of your bathtub, and run the water over it, as warm as you can stand it, until the tub is full. Soak in the tub, eyes closed, and reflect on how you'd like people to see you. As you do, say *I am confident, I am strong, I am beautiful, I am new, I am magical.*

Repeat this until the water has cooled, then get out of the tub and drain the water. Bury the bag in your yard.

March 10

War Water Spell
to Neutralize an Attack

You'll need:
- A jar with a lid
- Seven iron nails

The month of March is named for the war god Mars, who is often symbolized by iron and other metals of warfare. If someone has made it clear that you are enemies, the best defense is a good magical offense. Make a batch of war water and sprinkle it around your home or office to protect you from physical or psychic attacks. Try to do this on a Tuesday, which is associated with Mars and action in battle.

Collect rainwater in the jar during a thunderstorm — the more lightning, the better. After it's full, add the iron nails and close the lid. As you do, say *I am strong and I will fight, I will not be defeated.* Leave the jar with the water and the nails outside in the sun for seven days. You'll begin to notice that the nails are rusting and the water is turning brown. On the final day, sprinkle drops of the water around the places where your enemy tries to do you wrong — your office, your home, or anywhere else he or she may be lingering. As you sprinkle your war water, say *You have declared war upon me, but I will not let you harm me. You have made yourself my enemy, but you will not win.*

This should keep your enemy's attacks from being effective.

March 11

Spell to Overcome Challenges

You'll need:
- A purple candle
- Dirt gathered from three different crossroads intersections
- A red drawstring bag

In classical mythology, Herakles was the hero who overcame obstacles and challenges as part of his life journey. He was honored with a festival on March 11. If you've been facing some trials in your own life, this is a great day to do magic that will help you get past those hurdles. In some folk magic traditions, dirt gathered from a crossroads is used to unblock things that might be getting in your way. Use a purple candle to represent personal power.

Light the candle, and as you look into the flame, think about the specific obstacle you need to overcome. Do you need to conquer a fear? Take a risk you're unprepared for? Learn to deal with a medical issue? Be as focused as you possibly can. Place the dirt in the bag, mixing it all together, pull the drawstring tight, and say *I am successful and I am strong. My fears do not define me. Obstacles do not stop me. Challenges do not frighten me. I am successful and I am strong.*

Carry the bag with you, either in your pocket or in your purse, when you go out to take on the world.

March 12

Spell to Enhance Knowledge and Wisdom

You'll need:
- A yellow candle
- Nine almonds

Hypatia of Alexandria was the best-known philosopher and mathematician of her time, and she paid for her knowledge with her life. Martyred sometime in mid-March (the exact date is not clear), to this day she remains a symbol of knowledge, wisdom, and the power of the female mind. Today is the perfect time to do a spell to enhance your own intellectual abilities. Try to work this spell on a Wednesday, which is associated with study and learning. You'll be using a yellow candle and almonds, both of which are tied to intellect.

Find a quiet place to sit and do this working undisturbed, and light the candle. Focus on the flame, and consider all the ways you wish to expand your intellect. Do you want to do better in school? Perhaps learn a new skill? Maybe you just want a better understanding of the world around you. Think about your goal, and as you do, eat the almonds one at a time. With each one, say *I open my mind to new knowledge, I open my mind to wisdom, I open my mind to clarity, I open my mind to learning.*

When you have eaten all nine almonds, extinguish the candle.

March 13

Fire Spell for Good to Triumph Over Evil

You'll need:
- A black candle
- A white candle
- Sea salt

The Hindu festival of Holi falls in March, and is observed with great celebration, including giant bonfires. In addition to marking the beginning of spring, it is a time to celebrate the triumph of light over darkness and good over evil. In addition to the cleansing power of fire, this spell also calls for salt, which has been used for centuries as a method of purification and cleansing.

Begin by lighting the black candle. Look into the flame, and sprinkle half the salt around the candle. As you do, say *Evil, unhappiness, and negativity I banish, sadness and hatred now shall vanish.* Do this three times, and extinguish the candle.

Light the white candle, and the sprinkle the remaining salt around it, saying *Happiness, goodness, and positivity, these three things I call to me.*

Allow the white candle to burn out on its own, but take the black one far from your home to dispose of it.

82

March 14

Birch Bark Spell
to Heal a Broken Heart

You'll need:
- A blue pen
- A piece of birch bark

The birch tree, which is often associated with the spring equinox season, is sometimes seen as a symbol of new life. In a burned area, birch trees are typically the first ones to grow back, representing creation in the midst of what was destroyed. In folk magic, the bark is sometimes used to heal wounds, particularly burns. Take advantage of the magical properties of birch bark to help heal a broken heart.

Find a quiet place to sit near a moving body of water—a stream, creek, or even the ocean. Write the name of the person who broke your heart on the inside of the birch bark. Take a moment to hold the bark in your hands, and think about the good times you had together, but recognize that it is now over. Allow yourself the privilege of a good cry if you need to. Tear the birch bark into small pieces, and drop them, one at a time, into the water, saying *What once was has ended, and now I move on. I wish you the best that life has to offer, and now I move forward.*

After the birch bark has floated out of sight, go home and begin the next chapter of your life.

March 15

Earth Spell
to Help a Sick Pet

You'll need:
- A handful of dirt from your yard,
  or wherever your pet plays
- Rosemary, fresh or dried
- Eucalyptus leaves

Those of us who have pets know they are part of our families. We love them to the point of distraction, and it's devastating when they are sick or injured. Animals that feel unwell may exhibit signs of aggression as a response to pain; it's their way of telling us how they feel. This simple earth spell is a great way to send calming magic toward your pet. In addition, be sure to have a veterinarian evaluate any medical issues. Do this spell at sunrise.

Blend the dirt, the rosemary, and the eucalyptus* in a bowl. As you do, stir it clockwise to mix, saying *Health and wellness, from nose to tail, light and love will prevail. Calming magic, to you from me, as I will, so it shall be.* Place the mixture on a high shelf over your pet's crate, bed, or wherever he or she normally sleeps.

*Eucalyptus is toxic to dogs, so do not leave this blend in a place where your pet could ingest it.

March 16

Passion and Fertility Magic

You'll need:
- Three red candles
- A drum • A raw egg in a bowl

Libera was a classical fertility goddess, much like a female version of Bacchus or Dionysus. Her festival was observed every year on March 16–17, and included offerings from women who were having trouble conceiving because the passion in their marriages had dwindled. If you're struggling to conceive for this reason, and not because of underlying medical issues for which you should seek a doctor's treatment, try this spell to revive the heat in your relationship. Do this working in your bedroom at sundown.

Light the three candles on the table or nightstand closest to the bed. Say *Passion, desire, romance, and lust, the two us bound by love and trust. Candles bright, candles burn, it's time for passion to return.*

Walk around the perimeter of the bedroom in a clockwise direction, pounding rhythmically on the drum, saying *Burning love, burning desire, burning passion, burning fire in time to the beat.* Once you've circled the room three times, stop drumming. Crack the egg in the bowl, and mix it up with your finger so the yolk is broken. Dip your finger in the beaten egg and use it to draw a heart on the headboard and footboard of your bed, as you say *From head to toe and toe to head, passion return back to this bed. Wrapped entwined, never to part, two lovers joined, heart to heart.*

Extinguish the candles, and dispose of the egg outside, under your bedroom window.

March 17

Shamrock Spell
for Good Luck

You'll need:
- A gold candle
- A plate or glass candleholder
- A shamrock or four-leaf clover

The shamrock has long been a symbol of good luck and blessings, so March 17 is a perfect time to work a bit of magic to bring fortune your way! The shamrock is a specific type of clover with three leaves, but you can also use a four-leaf clover in this spell if you're fortunate enough to find one.

Light the candle, and place it on the plate on top of the shamrock. Watch the flames dance, and imagine the good fortune you'd like to see in your life. As the wax begins to melt, tilt the candle a bit so the wax runs down and drips on the shamrock's leaves. As it does, say *Luck locked in, night and day, luck sealed in place, and coming my way.*

Once the entire shamrock is coated in wax, allow it to cool. After the wax has hardened, place the shamrock under the welcome mat by your front door to invite luck into your home.

March 18

Tulip Spell
for Empowerment

You'll need:
- Three tulips with stems
- A mixing bowl or mortar and pestle
- A bottle of water with a cap

Come March, you'll begin to see signs of early spring flowers, including the tulip. Its bright petals appear in every shade you can imagine, and it is associated with prosperity and power. Wear a red tulip close to your heart to draw love, luck, and abundance. Do this personal empowerment working first thing in the morning, as the sun rises, preferably on a Sunday.

Tear the petals off the tulips slowly, and add them to the bowl. As you drop them in the bowl, say *I am happy, healthy, and whole. The sun gives me strength. I have power over my world.* After you've dropped all the petals in the bowl, tear the stems into small pieces and add them as well, saying *I am sturdy and resilient. The earth gives me stability. I have control over my world.*

Mash the flowers and stems into a paste, and add them to the bottle of water. Cap it, shake well, and leave it out in the sun for three days. Splash some tulip water on your wrists when you're in need of an empowerment boost.

March 19

Owl Spell
for Wise Choices

You'll need:
- A statue or picture of an owl
- Two pieces of gold paper and a pen
- A pendulum

March 19 is one of the days dedicated to Athena, known not only for her gift of strategy in battle, but also her wisdom. She is symbolized by the owl—also a creature of wisdom—so this is a good day to evaluate your decision-making process. Use a bit of owl magic to help yourself choose wisely between two options. If possible, do this working on a Wednesday, which is connected to wisdom.

Place the owl statue in front of you on a table. On the gold papers, write your two options. Hold the pendulum in your dominant hand over the two choices, one at a time. As you're watching the pendulum, say *Wise choices must be made, decisions for the best must be reached. Guide me toward the option that is right.*

When you see which option causes the pendulum to swing most, you'll know that's the wisest choice.

March 20

Apple Blossom Spell for Fidelity

You'll need:
- An apple branch with buds or blossoms on it
- A rose quartz stone
- A photo of you and your lover
  happy together

Iduna was a goddess who tended the apple orchards, and in some traditions she is celebrated around the time of the spring equinox. This is the season when the apple blossoms are just beginning to form on the trees, and they are associated not only with youth and immortality, but also love and fidelity. Today is a good day to do a working that establishes loyalty and faithfulness in a new relationship.

Place the rose quartz on top of the photo, but leave the faces visible. Focus on the photo, seeing the two of you happy, side by side. Slowly pluck the apple blossoms from the branch, rub them between your fingertips, and scatter them over the photo. As you do this, say *Love and faith and fidelity, truth and hope and loyalty. Mutual trust from you to me, and from me to you, so it shall be.*

Sleep with the photo, the stone, and the apple blossoms under your pillow.

March 21

Aries Spell to Add Excitement to Your Life

You'll need:
- Metal ball bearings
- A large horseshoe magnet

In the Zodiac, the sign of Aries begins on March 21. This is a fiery sign often associated with magnetic personalities, adventure, and leadership. Whether you're just trying to get through another humdrum day at work or you're seeking real adventure, take advantage of Aries energy to bring a little more excitement into your life. If possible, do this working in the seven days before a full moon.

Arrange the ball bearings in a circle. Take the time to play with them a little, and think about the sort of excitement you'd like in your life. Do you want to travel? Find fun new friends? Perhaps you just need some variation on the routines of everyday life. Focus on what you want as you arrange the ball bearings. Once you have them in place—and they may be rolling around a bit—hold the magnet in your dominant hand. Slowly move it toward the ball bearings, so they gradually begin to move toward the magnet. As they do, say *Adventure and fun is what I crave, I need excitement in my days. Enjoyment of life, come to me, as I will, so it shall be.*

Once all the ball bearings have connected to the magnet, put them someplace safe where they can't be disturbed.

March 22

Spring Equinox Egg Defense

You'll need:
- A marker
- A raw egg

Around March 22, the spring equinox falls, and it's a period of equal hours of darkness and light. It's a time of balance, and few things are as representative of life as the egg. In many folkloric traditions, it's the perfect magical symbol. If you're feeling off-kilter, it's possible that someone is sending negative thoughts or malicious energy your way. To make it stop, set up a defense system using a plain egg in its shell. Try to do this spell on a Sunday, which is tied to protection magic.

Write your name on the egg's shell. You can also add a drawing of your face, or identifiers like your birthdate or phone number. As you do, say *I name you [*YOUR NAME*], to stand in for me, absorbing any negativity. From yolk to white, to outer shell, be a decoy, so I'll be well.*

Place the egg in a spot where it will not be disturbed. If it begins to rot, dispose of it and replace it with a new one until the danger of negative energy has passed.

March 23

Sun Spell to Eliminate Your Stress

You'll need:
- A piece of yellow paper and a pen

In some Norse magical traditions, March 23 is the day of the festival known as the Summer Finding. It is a way to celebrate the end of winter, mark the return of new life, and recognize the power of the sun. There's a lot to be said for a bright, sunny afternoon following the long, dark days, so if you have a day when the sun is shining—even if it's cold—do this spell to help eliminate some of your winter stress. Try to do it as the sun goes down.

Find the highest point in your community that you can get to—a hilltop or a tall building works well. Once you arrive, write down the things that are stressing you out, repeating them until the paper is filled with your writing. Hold the paper high up in the air, toward the sun, and say *Power of the sun, warmth and light, I shed my stress this chilly night. Worries and cares that bother me, I send away, so it shall be.*

Tear the paper into the tiniest possible pieces, and throw them in the direction of the sun. As they blow away, watch your anxieties and stressors disappear with the setting sun.

March 24

Storm Moon Spell for Renewal of Energy

You'll need:
- A silver candle
- A bowl of rainwater collected during a storm
- A white glass bottle with a cap

March's full moon is known as the Storm Moon—and no wonder, considering all the windy, wet weather this month! The Storm Moon is associated with rebirth and renewal, so take advantage of this month's stormy magic and full moon vitality, and do a quick spell to revitalize your own energy levels. Do this spell outside at night, when the moon is at its fullest.

Light the candle, and watch as the shadows dance around you. Hold the bowl of water high so the moonlight is reflected in it. Say *Power of the moon, power of the rain, revitalize the power of my spirit. As the light shines upon me, may the energy of the storm moon lift me, give me life, and let my spirit soar.*

Pour the rainwater into the bottle and cap it. When you feel your energy lagging, anoint your wrists or behind your neck with the rainwater that the moon has blessed.

March 25

Spell to Take Back Your Life From an Internet Troll

You'll need:
• A photo of the person, or a piece of paper with his or her email address or screen name
• Flash drive or CD
• A hammer

We've all encountered these people online—often referred to as trolls, they're the ones who follow us all over the Internet, deliberately seeking us out so they can harass us. While you should report any threats or hints of illegal activity to the authorities immediately, you can also do this spell to reclaim some semblance of control over your online life. Do this working late at night, after dark.

Wrap the photo or paper tightly around the flash drive or CD. As you do, say *You can't control me in cyberspace, your connection to me will be erased.* Place the wrapped disc on a hard surface, and (wearing safety glasses for protection!)use the hammer to smash it to bits, saying *No more trolling, you're now defeated, your access to me has been deleted.*

Dispose of the smashed disc and shredded paper in the most foul-smelling trash bin you can find, far away from your home.

March 26

Spell for
Community Unity

You'll need:
- A blue piece of paper and a pen
- A white candle

In Hawaii, March 26 is celebrated as Prince Kūhiō Day, in honor of Prince Jonah Kūhiō Kalanianaʻole, a member of the Hawaiian royal family who later became a territorial delegate to Congress. It is often observed as a time to celebrate the community at large, and to do things for others by way of civic service. This is a perfect day to do a spell for unity. Whether you focus locally, globally, or on a single organization to which you belong, do this working to give a little magical boost to those who have to work together for the greater good.

Write down the name of the community, country, or organization to which you wish to send unifying magic, and fold the paper three times. Place it under the candle. Light the candle, and say *Healing and wisdom and unity, blessings of community, rid of us negativity, I send this healing gift from me.*

Allow the candle to burn out on its own, and when it has, leave it somewhere centrally located to the community you wish to help.

March 27

Fire Purification Spell

You'll need:
- A bonfire
- Bay leaves
- A black marker or a pen

The Persian festival of Nowruz falls around the time of the spring equinox. The word Nowruz comes from two Persian words meaning "new day," and it's a time to mark the rebirth of the land as the first day of the Iranian calendar. Often associated with fire and purification, Nowruz is a season of spring cleaning—take advantage of this, and use a bit of fire to do some purification magic. Try to do this spell on a Monday, which is associated with cleansing.

Start by doing a complete physical house cleaning—dust your tabletops and furniture, sweep everything from top to bottom, and clean the windows to let the sun shine in. Gather the contents of your dustpan (or vacuum canister), and place the detritus into your fire pit or fireplace. Get a good blazing fire going, and on the bay leaves, write the things that discourage you or are toxic to your life—like sadness, anger, doubt, or frustration. Hold the bay leaves in your hand, and say *I shed these things that are harmful to my soul, I am free of these things that stifle my spirit, I burn these things that discourage my heart. I send them away with the purifying power of fire, to haunt me no more.*

Throw the bay leaves into the fire and watch them burn. As they do, say good-bye to them forever.

March 28

Spell to Honor Your Ancestors

You'll need:
- Photos of your ancestors, or family heirlooms
- A charcoal incense disk in a fireproof bowl
- Dried rosemary

During the heyday of the Roman Empire, March 28 was the day of a festival called the Sacrifice at the Tombs. It was when families gathered together at their ancestral tombs to honor those who came before them, going back generations. Today many of us live far from the graves of our family members, but you can do a modern version of this celebration with a simple spell that calls upon your ancestors to watch over you. Use rosemary, which is associated with remembrance, in this working.

Arrange the photos or heirlooms on a flat surface so you can see all of them. Light the charcoal disk in the bowl, and add the rosemary on top of it to burn. Take a moment to sit back and enjoy the scent, and think about all the good memories of your ancestors. Focus on the photos and heirlooms, and say *Ancestors, blood of my blood, you whose spirit runs through me, I call upon you to watch over me. Keep me safe, keep me whole, keep me healthy, keep me strong. I ask that you protect me and guide me, so that I may make you proud.*

Once the rosemary has burned away, put the photos and heirlooms in a place of honor in your home.

March 29

Spell to Cope with Sudden Loss

You'll need
- Symbols of the four elements:
a rock, a feather, a candle, and a cup of water
- A photo of the person or pet you have lost

Tragically, many of us find ourselves facing sudden loss. Perhaps we lose a family member, a friend, or even a beloved pet without warning. This spell can help you say farewell to the person or pet who has passed, and allow you to begin healing from your grief. If possible, do this working at sunset.

Find a peaceful place outdoors where you can work undisturbed. Place the rock to the north to represent earth and the feather at the east to symbolize air. Light the candle, and place it to the south, representing fire, and the cup of water to the west. Begin by facing north, holding the photo, and turn in a clockwise direction as you say *[NAME], I send you now, back to the north, to the earth from which we spring. [NAME], I send you now, back to the east, to the air that gave you breath. [NAME], I send you now, back to the south, to the fire that drove your passion. [NAME], I send you now, back to the west, to the water from which cleanses your spirit.*

Hold the photo up to the setting sun, and say *I send you on your way, and you are gone but not forgotten. You will always live within my heart, and someday, we will meet again.*

As the sun drops beyond the horizon, extinguish the candle, and bury it along with the rock, the feather, and the water. Take the photo home and keep in a place of honor.

March 30

Earth Spell to Reconnect with Nature

You'll need:
• A spoon or small trowel • A glass jar
• A small clipping of your own hair

I n the classical world, this was a time of year to celebrate the goddess Concordia, who often represented the connection between mankind and the natural world. In the spring, the earth is beginning to show signs of new life, so this is a great time to get outside and do a working to reconnect with nature. Do this outdoors on a sunny day.

Find a place that represents nature—whether it's a secluded spot in the woods, an empty stretch of beach, or even just your own backyard. When you get there, take a few moments to enjoy the silence. Breathe in the fresh air, turn your face up to the sun, and feel the soft ground beneath your feet. When you're completely relaxed, dig a small hole with the spoon. As you do, say *Earth I am connected to, earth I am joined to, earth I am linked to.* Place some of the soil in the jar.

Next, place the hair clipping into the hole, and use the remainder of the soil to cover it back up, saying *I leave here a link to myself, I leave here a piece of my spirit, I leave here a part of me.* Sit as long as you like, feeling the connection linking you to that patch of soil or sand. When you're ready, take your jar home and keep it where you can see it each day as a reminder of your bond with the land.

March 31

Quick Spell to Control Your Tongue

You'll need:
- A freezer-safe container
- Vinegar

W e've all found ourselves saying something we immediately felt bad about, often in response to something a loved one said or did to us. While it can be satisfying to lash out, we almost always wish we hadn't. This quick spell comes in handy when you can feel angry words making their way from your brain to the tip of your tongue, and will help you stop yourself from saying things you'll regret.

Fill the container with vinegar, and as you do, say *Cool my words, cool my voice, cool my tongue. I will think before I speak, I will pause before I harm, I will consider the damage that my words can do.* Place the container in the freezer, and leave it there for as long as you need to.

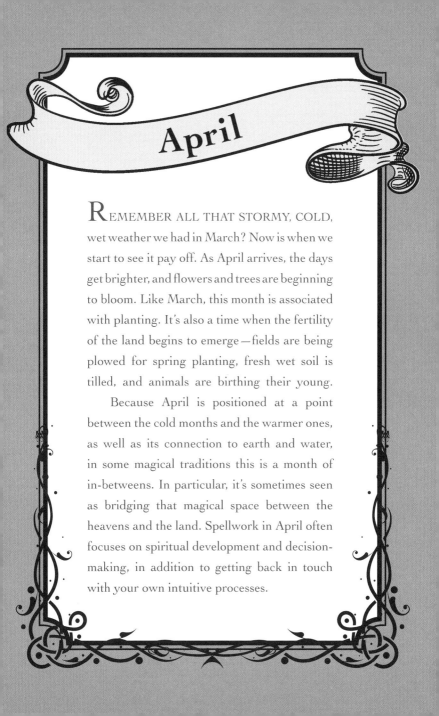

April

Remember all that stormy, cold, wet weather we had in March? Now is when we start to see it pay off. As April arrives, the days get brighter, and flowers and trees are beginning to bloom. Like March, this month is associated with planting. It's also a time when the fertility of the land begins to emerge—fields are being plowed for spring planting, fresh wet soil is tilled, and animals are birthing their young.

Because April is positioned at a point between the cold months and the warmer ones, as well as its connection to earth and water, in some magical traditions this is a month of in-betweens. In particular, it's sometimes seen as bridging that magical space between the heavens and the land. Spellwork in April often focuses on spiritual development and decision-making, in addition to getting back in touch with your own intuitive processes.

April 1

Spider Spell
to Reveal a Liar

You'll need:
- Silver embroidery floss
- A white candle

As spring approaches, spiders begin to emerge with the warmer weather. Their tangled webs can come in very handy if you think someone may be lying to you, but you can't quite determine who it is, or what part of a story is true. Most spiders haven't finished building their webs—and when they do, they need them to live in—but you can make your own tangled web to compel liars to reveal themselves. If possible, do this working on a Wednesday, which is associated with communication.

Separate the embroidery floss into individual strands. Begin knotting and tangling them together, and as you do, say *Tangled web and tangled weave, someone out there does deceive, tangled trap catching flies, reveal the person telling lies.*

Soon the liar will reveal his or her duplicity to everyone involved.

April 2

Diamond Spell
for Intuition

You'll need:
- A silver candle
- A diamond ring on a string or a chain
- A notebook or a journal

April's birthstone is the diamond, which is traditionally associated with engagements and marriage, but is also used in spellwork related to intuition. If you've ever thought you might like to develop your own psychic abilities, or learn to better trust your gut feelings, do this working during the waxing gibbous moon phase in the seven days prior to the full moon. Perform this spell at night, right before you go to bed.

Light the candle, and gaze into the flame. As you do, slowly raise the diamond ring so it appears in your peripheral vision, saying *Diamond sparkling in the light, diamond magic in the night, show me what I need to see, visions appearing in dreams for me. Intuition comes as the moonlight grows, as above, so below.*

As the candlelight reflects in the diamond, you may start to see images appear—there may be things you're not sure about, but that's okay. Gradually bring the diamond up so it is at eye level, and continue watching. When you feel like you're no longer seeing anything, extinguish the candle and go to bed. Keep the journal nearby so when you wake up, you can write down and analyze the visions that appeared in the candlelight and in your dreams.

April 3

Dandelion Spell to Make a Wish

You'll need:
• Dandelions that have gone to seed

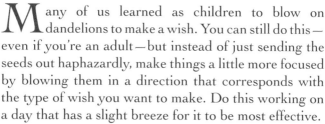

Many of us learned as children to blow on dandelions to make a wish. You can still do this — even if you're an adult — but instead of just sending the seeds out haphazardly, make things a little more focused by blowing them in a direction that corresponds with the type of wish you want to make. Do this working on a day that has a slight breeze for it to be most effective.

To do this very basic spell, first determine which direction to blow the seeds. For wishes related to stability, security, and the home, face north. If your wish relates to communication or the powers of the mind, turn to the east. South is connected to matters of the heart and strong will, and west is associated with purification and cleansing. Finally, keep in mind that if your wish involves bringing something to you, blow into the wind, but if you want to get rid of something, blow with the wind.

Face the appropriate direction, and say *I send these seeds into the air, carrying my wish I know not where, traveling about on the breeze, as I will, so it shall be.* Take a deep breath, and slowly blow the dandelion seeds off the stem. When you're done, bury the stem near your front door.

April 4

Spell to Protect Children When They Are Away

You'll need:
- A yellow candle
- A cloth doll to represent the child
- A piece of your own clothing, worn but not washed

April 4 was the day of the festival of Cybele, also known as Magna Mater, the great mother. Fiercely protective in her role as a giver of life, she was often invoked by mothers to watch over children in times of danger. Parents today—both mothers and fathers—are often anxious about letting kids out of their sight. Do this very basic spell to protect your child when he or she is at school, at a relative's house, or visiting friends.

Light the candle, and wrap the doll in the piece of clothing. Hold the doll in your arms, as you would your child, and say *I name you [CHILD'S NAME], and I will care for you. I will wrap you in my arms, surround you with my love, and protect you until my last breath. You are mine, and I will always watch over you, even when you are not at my side.*

Extinguish the candle. Keep the doll in a safe place, and when your child is away from home, be sure to give the doll a kiss as a reminder of your protective love.

April 5

Gambler's Lucky Dice Spell

You'll need:
- A green candle
- A pair of standard dice
- A piece of gold cloth

The goddess Fortuna was celebrated on April 5, and she is associated with good luck, particularly in matters of gambling and random bits of chance. If you enjoy games of risk, whether you're playing for fun or high stakes, try this spell to bring a little extra good fortune your way.

Light the candle, and place the dice beside it so the numbers facing up equal seven—it doesn't matter if you use 5 + 2, 3 + 4, or 6 + 1, because seven is considered a lucky number in any combination. As the candle wax begins to melt, drip a bit on the tops of the dice, then push them together so the numbers that total seven are connected by the wax. Say *Lucky dice, lucky sevens, lucky numbers, may fortune follow me.* Wrap the connected dice in the cloth, and carry it in your pocket at the gaming tables.

April 6

Crocus Spell for
New Love Dream Magic

You'll need:
- Two crocus flowers with stems
- Pink or red thread

As the days begin to warm in early April, one of the first flowers you'll see is the crocus, which is often associated with newly blooming love. The crocus is also known to enhance visions and bring about intuitive dreams. Why not combine both intentions and do a working to dream about your future love life? If possible, do this on a Friday.

Find a quiet place to sit away from other people — a park, the banks of a stream, or out in the woods. Think about the attributes you'd like a future lover to have. Do you want someone who is sensitive and thoughtful? Perhaps you prefer a lover who has a great sense of humor, or one who is free-spirited and adventurous. Use the thread to bind the crocuses together, wrapping the stems, and say *Two become one, tied together, show me the one who will love me forever.*

Place the crocuses beneath your pillow that night, and your future love will appear to you in a dream.

April 7

Spell to Move on From Your Past

You'll need:
- A black candle
- A blue candle
- A white candle

We've all done things that have impacted us in a negative way, and sometimes it's hard to move on from those choices. If your past is preventing you from being happy in the present, do this spell to clear your way. Try to do this working at sunrise.

Light the black candle, and say *I send away my pain, I send away my guilt, I send away that which has damaged me. It has no power over me, and I send away my past.*

Next, light the blue candle. Say *I am healed, I am strong, I am worthy. My past is gone, and I permit myself to live in the present.*

Light the white candle, saying *My soul is pure, my soul is fresh, my soul is cleansed. Every day is a new day, and the future is bright.*

Extinguish the candles, and know that your past can no longer hold you back.

April 8

Button Spell to Release An Obsession

You'll need:
- Blue fabric
- Needle and thread
- Thirteen black buttons

Do you have an obsession that you just can't shake? Someone or something that consumes every thought and waking moment? Recognizing our own addictions and obsessions is the first step to moving beyond them, but sometimes a little magical nudge can help us break free. This spell takes thirteen days to complete.

On one edge of the fabric, stitch the buttons in a line, evenly spaced. While you're doing so, think about the thing or person that has become your obsession. On the fabric's opposite edge, make thirteen buttonholes. Fasten all thirteen buttons into their corresponding holes. Each day, unbutton one of them, and as you do, say *You are out of my head, out of my heart, out of my mind. I release you from my thoughts, and I release myself from my obsession. You have no power over me.*

After the thirteenth button has been released, take the fabric far away to dispose of it, and never think of your obsession again.

April 9

New Home Blessing Spell

You'll need:
- A bundle of sage
- A brand-new welcome mat

Spring is the most popular time of year for home buying, and it's always exciting to move into new digs! However, before you start filling the place with your stuff, it's not a bad idea to do a bit of magical cleansing. Purifying the interior, along with a simple threshold blessing, can create a symbolic doorway to the home that keeps negative energy out while allowing positive energy to come inside.

Start by doing a physical cleaning of the new house, working in a clockwise direction—after all, who knows what the previous owners have left behind? Once you've done this, light the sage and walk through the house—again, in a clockwise direction—smudging the entire home. As you work your way around each room, say *Love and light in this home, blessings and abundance in this home, joy and happiness in this home.*

After you've finished the inside of the home, do the same thing on the outside, starting and ending at the front door. Finally, place the new welcome mat on the front step, and say *Love and light are welcome here, blessings and abundance are welcome here, joy and happiness are welcome here.*

Leave the sage outside the front door to burn out on its own.

April 10

Snakeskin Spell
for Spiritual Growth

You'll need:
- Sandalwood incense
- A snakeskin
- A small cloth pouch

Snakes shed their skins regularly, and if you spend any time outdoors, you may have encountered a shed. Next time you see one, pick it up—snakeskin is associated with transformation in some forms of folk magic. Do you feel like you're just not motivated lately? Maybe you've lost your connection to the Divine. If you feel like you've been stuck in a rut spiritually or emotionally, try this working to give you a little magical jump-start.

Light the incense, and take a few minutes to think about your spiritual path and where you'd like it to go eventually. Hold the snakeskin between your palms, and gently rub it in a circular motion, saying *Change, transformation, growth, and evolution. I shed the old me and welcome my new self. I am a divine and spiritual being, and I welcome the journey to my new destination.*

Place the snakeskin in the pouch, and carry it in your pocket until you feel you've regained your lost spiritual ground.

April 11

Toilet Paper Spell to Get Rid of a Bully

You'll need:
- Nine squares of toilet paper
- A black pen

Ever have someone in your life who is acting like a bully? Maybe it's the coworker in the next cubicle who wants your job. Perhaps it's a creepy ex who can't let go. It might even be your next-door neighbor. This spell is very simple, and it's extremely gratifying to do when you're dealing with bullying behavior. In addition to this working, be sure to report bullying actions to the proper authorities or supervisors if need be.

Write the bully's name three times on each of the nine squares of toilet paper. Sit down on the toilet, do your business, and then use the toilet paper to wipe. Drop it in the toilet and flush. As the toilet paper goes down, say *[*BULLY'S NAME*], I have no use for you. You have as much value to me as this toilet paper, and now you're out of my life. Be gone, be gone, be gone for good!*

Wash your hands, and enjoy the rest of your day.

April 12

Grain Spell
for Abundance

You'll need:
- A pot of soil
- Seven pennies
- Seven seeds for corn, wheat, or other grains

April 12 was a time to celebrate Ceres, a goddess of the grain fields—her name gives us the word *cereal*. She was associated primarily with the spring planting season, when the grain was sown to be reaped during the harvest months. By putting seeds in now, you're laying the foundation for abundance later in the year. Do this spell on a sunny day in the week before the full moon.

Use your finger to poke seven holes in the soil. In each hole, place a penny and a seed, side by side, and cover them up. Say *Earth and air, sun and rain, increase for me abundance and gain. Soil and wind, water and light, bring to me blessings bright.*

Add water, and place the pot in a sunny window. When the seedlings grow large enough, transfer them to your garden.

April 13

Easter Lily Anti-Love Spell

You'll need:
- Three black candles
- Three Easter lilies

This time of year, Easter lilies are in full bloom just about everywhere. The bulbs and flowers are toxic, and in many forms of folk magic they come in very handy to counteract love spells that someone might be sending your way. You can even use this working if you think someone else might be the target of a love spell.

Find a place with moving water, like a stream or river. Place the candles on a flat surface, and light them, saying *I will banish the love, banish the magic, banish the spell that binds me*. Pluck a petal from one of the Easter lilies, and drop it into the water. As you do, say *[*PERSON'S NAME**], your love spell is gone*. When the petal has floated completely out of your sight, repeat this until all the petals are gone from the Easter lilies. When you are done, extinguish the candles, and bury them—along with the stems—somewhere far from your home.

> * *If you don't know specifically who has placed a love spell on you, that's okay. Substitute the name of the person with* "You that have cast upon me" *instead.*

April 14

Spring Cleaning
Broom Blessing Spell

You'll need:

- A broom
- Colored ribbons — use spring colors like yellow, green, and purple — and bells
- Your choice of other adornments

In many magical traditions, the broom is a witch's most practical tool. It can be used to sweep out all kinds of negative energy, while sweeping positive blessings inward. If you have a broom, you can incorporate this spell into your spring cleaning to give your home not only a sense of physical tidiness, but also metaphysical cleansing.

Decorate your broom with the ribbons and bells. As you wrap the ribbons around the broom's handle, say *Spring is here, winter's away, I sweep blessings around my home today. Wrapping ribbons to bring spring in, harmony and magic come within.* Add the bells so when you move the broom, you'll hear them ringing.

Sweep each room in a counterclockwise direction, beginning and ending with the doorway. As you sweep, say (or even sing!) *Clean and clear, welcome spring, bristles sweep and bells will ring. Blessings this sunny day so fine, to my home, to me, and mine!*

Once you've swept each room, sweep all the dust and dirt outside so the breeze can blow it out of your life. Hang the broom on your door as a reminder of the blessings in your home.

April 15

Magical Money
Mojo Spell

You'll need:
- A green candle
- A gold marker or gold paint
  and a paintbrush
- A flat stone

It's April 15, and if you live in the United States, you know what that means: It's the deadline for filing your income tax. If you're lucky enough to be getting a refund, congratulations! If you're not that fortunate, it never hurts to do a bit of money magic to bring a few extra dollars your way. Try to time this working so it's during the seven days prior to the full moon.

Light the candle, and use the marker or paint to create dollar signs all over both sides of the stone, covering as much of it as you can. As you do this, imagine the stone attracting more money into your life—you might even want to think about what you'll do with the funds that come your way! As you create the symbols, say *Money come, come to me, life filled with prosperity, I paint this stone to plant the seed, draw the money that I need.*

After you're done, place the stone under the candle, and allow it to sit for seven minutes. Each night for the next week, light the candle and let it burn for seven more minutes. Money should begin to trickle back into your life.

April 16

Spring Weeding Spell

You'll need:
• Gardening tools like a hoe,
a shovel, and gloves
• Paper bags

By mid-April, many of us are beginning to plan our gardens, and it's a good time to clear your plots of spring weeds and other overgrowth that formed during the winter. If you have some spiritual overgrowth you need to tend to right now, use this spell to work on your garden and your spirit at the same time.

Begin working your way around the garden in a clockwise direction, using the hoe and shovel to loosen the soil, and pulling up weeds and rocks. As you do so, toss the detritus into the bags, and say *Inch by inch, row by row, clearing a space for seeds to grow. Earth and soil, sun and rain, my soul and spirit are clear again.*

Repeat this, as you work your way around the garden space, until you've cleared away everything. Put out the bags of debris to be hauled away with your regular trash pickup.

April 17

Spell to Adopt the Dog You Want

You'll need:
- A piece of paper and a pen
- A leash
- A food bowl

If you've ever wanted to have a dog in your life, spring is a great time to adopt. You may have already thought about what qualities you'd like to see in a canine companion—do you want a family-friendly pet? One that lives comfortably in an apartment? Perhaps you want a high-energy running partner! Before you go to a shelter to see who's available for you to love, do this working to help you find the right pet to come live with you.

Make a list of seven characteristics you'd like to see in your new dog. Write down things like LOYAL, PLAYFUL, or PROTECTIVE. Once you've made your list, roll up the paper and wrap it with the leash, saying *A dog to love, a dog for life, a dog in times of joy and strife. I will find the dog that's mine, to care for forever, for all of time.*

Place the paper and leash in the bowl, and put it in a place where you can see it regularly. For the next seven days, greet the leash and paper when you walk by, saying *You're the dog for me, in my heart, once you're home, we'll never part.*

After a week has passed, go to the shelter or pet adoption agency, and find a companion to love.

April 18

Mud Mask
Spiritual Battle Spell

You'll need:
• Cosmetic mud or clay mask
• Water • A mirror

The Pictish peoples often painted themselves blue with dye from the woad plant prior to going into battle. This made them look especially fierce, and did a good job of scaring off enemies. If you find yourself facing spiritual challenges, do this working to give you a bit of an extra boost! Don't worry if you don't have access to woad dye (most people don't); this spell uses a mud mask, available from the cosmetics department at your local store.

Mix the mud or clay with a little water at a time until you've created a thick paste. Looking into the mirror, use a finger to paint designs on your face — spirals, lines, dots, symbols, and the like. You can even paint your arms, legs, or any other body part. As you do, say *I am a warrior, and I am fierce. I am mighty, and I am unstoppable. I am brave, and I will not be defeated, in this life or in the next.* Repeat this six times, for a total of seven, getting increasingly louder and more ferocious — by the seventh time you should be shouting into the mirror.

When you've finished, let out the most primal battle cry you can. Take a few moments to imagine yourself defeating your spiritual enemies, then hop in the shower to rinse away the clay.

April 19

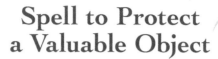

Spell to Protect a Valuable Object

You'll need:
- A bowl of water that has been left out in the moonlight
- A hematite stone
- An empty spritzer bottle

When you travel, hotels often tell you to store your valuables in their safe so they can't be held responsible for what happens to items left in your room. However, sometimes we have things of value that can't be locked up in a box. If something has sentimental value for you, use this spell to keep it away from those who might want to remove it from your possession.

Place the hematite stone in the bottom of the spritzer bottle, and add the water. As you do, say *Hematite stone, water of the moon, I blend you and consecrate you to protect that which is mine.*

Spritz the water all around the item you wish to protect. Say *Guard this [*ITEM*] from prying eyes, it belongs to me, and it is mine. None shall see, none shall covet, none shall take.*

Spray around the item and repeat the incantation for nine days.

April 20

Taurus Spell
for Reliability

You'll need:
- A brown candle
- Patchouli incense
- A bowl of soil

In the Zodiac, the month of Taurus the bull begins on April 20. Taurus is typically associated with reliability, steadfastness, and security. If you're worried that you've been letting people down lately and not picking up the slack where you should be, do this working to help inspire yourself to be more reliable and stable.

Light the candle and the incense, and take a few minutes to look at the flame and think about the ways you've failed to pull your weight recently. Are you ready to change things? Consider what you need to do—both mundane and magic—to make yourself more reliable. Put your hands in the soil, and say *Like the earth, I am grounded. Like the earth, I am stable. Like the earth, I am dependable. Those who love me can count on me. Those who know me may rely upon me. Those who need me know I am there for them always.*

Blow out the candle and empty the soil into your yard, and make the changes necessary to become a more reliable person.

April 21

Seed Moon Spell for Professional Advancement

You'll need:
- A gold candle • A calendar and a pen
- Gold adhesive stars

April's full moon is known as the Seed Moon, and it's a good time of year to think about what you want to cultivate for yourself professionally. Perhaps you're stuck in a rut at work. Maybe you got passed over for the last promotion, or you're thinking about a total career change. Take advantage of April's moon magic to plant the seeds of professional abundance that you can harvest later. Do this working on the night of the full moon.

Light the candle, and look at the calendar for the next three weeks. What are the mundane things you need to accomplish to succeed professionally? Do you need to complete a big project? Get an interview with your dream company? Mark the calendar accordingly, mapping out a timeline for professional growth. Place the candle on top of the calendar, and say *I am worthy, I am successful, I am moving up. I will be noticed, I will be acknowledged, I will be recognized. I will succeed, I will achieve my goals, and it will be my own doing.*

Each day, light the candle and let it burn for nine minutes. As you accomplish each of the tasks on your calendar, give yourself a gold star, and take credit for being the instrument of your own success.

April 22

Earth Day Spell to Help the Environment

You'll need:
- A tree seedling or sapling
- A shovel
- A small cloth bag

Each year, many of us observe Earth Day on April 22 by participating in community cleanups and trying to spread awareness of environmental issues. If this is something close to your heart, in addition to doing some hands-on work, do a bit of magical work to help out the planet. Work this spell on a sunny day.

Dig a hole large enough for the tree's root ball, and place the seedling or sapling in the hole. As you begin to fill it in, say *The earth is our mother, and she is sacred. The earth is our home, and it has value. With this tree, I plant my blessings. With this tree, I plant my wishes for a safe and healthy planet.*

Continue until the hole is completely filled in, and water the tree. Place a bit of the leftover soil in the cloth bag, and keep it in your home as a reminder that you are a steward of the environment.

April 23

Spell to Bless
an Unborn Baby

You'll need:
- A white candle
- A new receiving blanket
- Lavender

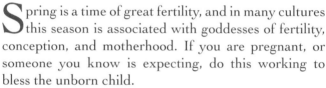

Spring is a time of great fertility, and in many cultures this season is associated with goddesses of fertility, conception, and motherhood. If you are pregnant, or someone you know is expecting, do this working to bless the unborn child.

Light the candle, and hold the blanket in your arms. If you can hold it against your bare skin, that's even better. Say *Bless this child who comes into my world, bless this child of mine. Bless this baby who's on its way, bless this baby, a gift from the Divine.*

Place the lavender in the center of the blanket, and carefully fold it up. Put the folded blanket in the baby's crib, and leave it there until he or she is born.

April 24

Hyacinth
Love Divination

You'll need:
- A pink candle
- A hyacinth stalk

The hyacinth is one of the most fragrant spring flowers, and it is usually blooming around the middle to the end of April. Each hyacinth stalk has dense clusters of multiple blossoms, so it can be a useful divination tool. If you've developed feelings for someone but you're not sure if they are reciprocated, use a hyacinth to get an idea of where you really stand.

Light the candle, and begin removing the individual blossoms from the stalk one at a time. As you do, count them off by threes, saying *Love is returned by love, love is returned by friendship, love is simply denied.*

The phrase you are saying when you pluck the final blossom will let you know if your feelings are returned.

April 25

Time Management Spell

You'll need:
- A blue candle
- A pocket watch
- A toothpick

Ever feel like the hours and days have gotten away from you? It happens a lot, especially if you are busy or easily distracted. Get yourself a bit more focused with this time management spell. Use an analog pocket watch with hands, rather than a digital one.

Light the candle, and watch the flame. Pay attention to your breathing, and imagine time slowing down as you inhale and exhale. Open the cover of the pocket watch. Dip the end of the toothpick in the melted candle wax, and use it to make an hourglass shape on the inside of the watch's cover. As you do, say *Time passes by, hands on the clock, stretching the hours, tick tock, tick tock.*

Keep in mind that an hourglass is shaped very much like an infinity symbol—you could be giving yourself all kinds of extra time to get things done! Carry the watch in your pocket, and whenever you realize you're wasting valuable time, open it up as a reminder to manage your time more effectively.

April 26

Spell to Help Calm an Anxious Child

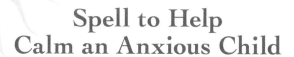

You'll need:
- Elastic cording
- Blue and gold pony beads

In many places, late April is the time for Take Your Child to Work Day. This is a great opportunity for kids to see what their parents do, but it can also be fairly stressful for children. After all, they're in an unfamiliar situation and surrounded by adults they don't know. Do this working the night before you take your child to your job—and, if possible, have your child participate in crafting the spell!

Cut a piece of elastic cording long enough to go around the child's wrist comfortably three times. String the beads, alternating colors, along the cording, and as you do, say *Blue and gold, gold and blue, calming energy from me to you*.

Once you've strung all the beads, knot the cording, and give it to your child to wear as a bracelet, wrapped three times around the wrist. If your youngster starts getting anxious, remind him or her to touch the beads and think about the calming energy you've sent that way.

April 27

Wind Chime Spell to Keep Away Trespassers

You'll need:
- Yellow ribbon
- Four small sets of wind chimes

In many magical traditions, bells and chimes are associated with the realm of mischievous fairies and the banishment of evil spirits. If someone in your neighborhood is being a nuisance and won't stay off your property, set up wind chimes as a magical barrier. Do this working on a Sunday, if possible.

Cut the ribbon into four lengths, and use it to hang the wind chimes at the four outside corners of your house, beginning at the front door and working in a clockwise direction. As you walk the perimeter, say *Chimes and bells, keep [NAME] from my home, bells and chimes, [NAME] leave us alone!*

Periodically replace the yellow ribbons as they get weathered.

April 28

The Happy-Ever-After Love Spell

You'll need:

- Some soil over which your lover has walked
- A small onion
- A planter or pot, never used

Love is a many-layered thing, and if you've recently embarked on a new love relationship, there's nothing wrong with giving it a little magical boost to help it flourish and grow.

Place the soil in the pot. Plant the onion, and cover it up. Add water, and as you do so, say *This little onion I command to grow, as the rain falls down and as wind blows. As the sun above shines and burns, [NAME]'s love toward me shall turn. With each layer of onion skin, [NAME]'s love for me shall grow within.*

Place the pot in a sunny spot at the south side of your house. The relationship will begin slowly, like the onion, and then strengthen and grow.

April 29

Arbor Day
Tree Healing Spell

You'll need:
- A jar of water that has been left in the sun all day
- A quartz crystal
- Dried sage

The last Friday of April is typically observed as Arbor Day, and it's a celebration that involves planting new trees. If you already have trees, but you've noticed they aren't doing so well, this is the perfect opportunity to do some healing magic on their behalf. Do this spell at night, after the sun has set.

Sit at the base of your tree, and place your hands on the trunk. Feel the life that flows through it, and listen to your intuition if it tells you this tree needs help. Place the crystal at the base of the trunk, pressing it into the soil, and say *I present you with healing magic, ground to sky, roots to leaves, trunk to branches.* Sprinkle the sage in a circle around the trunk, saying *I offer you love and cleansing, ground to sky, roots to leaves, trunk to branches.* Finally, pour the sun water around the trunk. Say *I give you water and the light of the sun, ground to sky, roots to leaves, trunk to branches. May you heal and recover, and feel the renewal of life once more.*

Periodically add more sun water and sage to the base of the tree as the season progresses.

April 30

Bonfire Spell to Protect Against Danger

You'll need:
• One yellow candle for
each member of your family
• Dried thistles
• Sea salt

In Germany, the night of April 30 is celebrated as Walpurgisnacht. Named for a saint, it is traditionally a time in which large bonfires are lit as protection against the forces of darkness. You don't need to build an enormous fire, but you can use candles to protect you and your loved ones against danger from sources both known and unknown. Do this working at night.

Light the candles, and as you do, call off the names of each family member you wish to protect. Arrange the candles in a circle, saying *Family bonds, love and light, flames protect us in the dark of night.* Place the thistles in a ring outside the candles, and say *Leaves and flowers and spikes and bristles, protection with these thorny thistles.* Finally, sprinkle the salt in a circle outside the thistles. *Salt surround us and keep us well, danger pass by the place we dwell.*

Allow the candles to burn out on their own, and in the morning, scatter the salt and the thistles around your front doorstep.

May

MAY IS A SEASON OF FERTILITY and new life—in fact, the month kicks off with Beltane, a fertility festival represented by the Maypole. This is the season in which the ground begins to warm, and the fresh earth opens up to receive the seeds for the year's crops. It's a time of strong masculine energy in many magical traditions, flowers are in bloom, and the dormant vegetation of last year is coming back to life.

This month is a reminder that the warm, sunny weeks of summer are just around the corner. Spellwork in May, in many magical traditions, is geared toward fire, fertility, and raw power.

May 1

Spring Seed
Blessing Spell

You'll need:
• Gardening tools
• Packets of seeds, or seedlings

If your geographical region is past the danger of frost, you may be lucky enough that you can plant your seeds directly in the ground on May 1. To ensure a successful garden this year, do this working when you put your seeds—or seedlings, if you started them in pots during the late winter—into the ground. If you don't have room for a full-size garden, don't worry. You can grow your herbs, flowers, and veggies in containers instead!

Use a shovel or hoe to loosen the soil, and don't be afraid to put your hands right into the earth. Take the time to connect with your land. Feel the loose soil beneath your feet, the sun in the sky, the warm on your face. Get down on the ground and use your fingers to make holes for your seeds. Drop a seed or two in each hole, and as you do, say *May the soil be blessed as the land grows warm, may these seeds be blessed as the earth becomes fruitful, bringing forth the garden anew.*

Cover each seed with the loose soil, and as you do, offer up a simple thanks for the bounty you'll be seeing in the coming months. Water your garden, and know that you've created something wonderful.

May 2

Violet Long-Distance Healing Spell

You'll need:
- Blue paper and a pen
- Violets with stems
- A white vase filled with water

By spring, violets are usually in bloom. This flower appears delicate but is actually fairly hardy, which makes it perfect for healing magic, especially when you have a friend or family member far away. You can do this any time, or when the need is greatest.

Write the name of the person who is ill nine times, and then wrap the paper snugly around the stems of the flowers. As you do, say *Healing and love from far away, I send you this magical blessing. Healing and love to your body, your mind, your soul. Healing and love from me to you across the miles.*

Slide the paper and the flowers into the vase, and place it in a sunny window. Don't forget to replenish the water as it evaporates.

May 3

Spell to Celebrate Female Friendship

You'll need:
• A bottle of wine (or grape juice) and glasses
• A bowl of honey blended with milk
• A bundle of sage

May 3 was the festival day of Bona Dea, the "good goddess." She was a fertility goddess honored by women in secret rituals that no man was permitted to gaze upon, and although there is little documentation as to the specifics, it is generally assumed that this was an opportunity for women to get out from under the watchful eyes of their husbands and fathers. Invite some girlfriends to join you for this spell to strengthen and celebrate the bonds of your friendship.

Invite your friends to sit on the floor in a circle. Pass the bowl of milk and honey around the circle. As each woman receives the bowl, ask her to take a sip, speak her name, and say *what has brought her to the group.* It can be as simple as *I am [NAME], and I am here because I love each of you.* Once the bowl has made its way around, light the sage bundle, and say *We are women, we are wise, we are wonderful. We are sisters, we are spiritual, we are strong. We are fearless, we are friends, we are family.*

Pour each friend a glass of wine and pass them around. When everyone has one, raise your glasses in a toast to the sisters of your heart.

May 4

Hawthorn Spell to Break a Curse

You'll need:
- A plump, juicy orange
- Nine thorns from a hawthorn tree

While most people go their entire lives without encountering curses or hexes, if things just don't seem to be going right for you, and the only explanation is a magical one, it's possible you might be the recipient of metaphysical mischief. If that's the case, it certainly won't hurt to break out a bit of self-defense. Use the spikes of the hawthorn tree to turn things around on the person sending negative energy your way.

Hold the orange in front of you, and speak directly to it, saying *You will not attack me, you will not harm me. I send back to you what you have sent to me. Your work has no power over me or mine, I return it to you, nine times nine.*

Use the thorns to pierce the skin of the orange, but take your time. Jab each one into the orange eight times, and then leave it in place on the ninth one. Once the orange has been punctured with all nine spikes, nine times each, take it somewhere far from your home to bury it, and think about it no more.

May 5

Emerald Spell for Fidelity

You'll need:
- Two pink candles
- An emerald ring or necklace

The traditional birthstone for the month of May is the emerald, which represents loyalty and fidelity. If you're concerned that a friend or family member may be toying with the idea of betrayal—either voluntarily or inadvertently—do this working to ensure he or she remains loyal and true.

Light the candles, and give each of them a name—one represents you, and the other stands for the person whose loyalty you may be questioning. Place them side by side so they are touching, and say *We are bonded, we are bound, we are tied by love and loyalty.*

Pass the emerald over the flames of the candles, saying *I deserve respect, I deserve fidelity, I deserve allegiance.* Give the ring or the necklace to the person as a gift to wear or to carry in their pocket as a talisman.

May 6

Protection Spell
for New Drivers

You'll need:
- A toy car that looks like your teen's vehicle
- A large sheet of bubble packing material
- Duct tape

If you're the parent of a teenage driver, very few things induce as much anxiety as watching him or her pull out of the driveway alone for the first time. While you can't be with your child every second of every day, you can certainly add an extra layer of magical protection when your new driver takes the keys in hand and rolls out of your sight.

Place the toy car in the center of the packing material, saying *You are protected and you are safe, you are shielded and you are sheltered.* Wrap the material around the car snugly, then wind the duct tape around it, saying *Safe from danger, safe from harm, you are protected.*

Once you have wrapped the entire thing securely with the tape, store it in the trunk of the vehicle your teen is driving.

May 7

Spell to Say Farewell to a Deceased Pet

You'll need:
- A pink candle
- Two stones, one to represent you and one to represent your pet
- Symbols of the four elements: earth, air, fire, and water*

The loss of a pet can be traumatic and devastating. They are, after all, part of our families, and we love them unconditionally. Once a pet passes away, it can be hard to move on from the grief. Do this spell to help ease the transition after your pet has died.

Light the candle, and hold the stones together in your hand, remembering the love you felt for your pet. Think about the wonderful times you had together, and the joy you shared—it's okay to cry if you need to. When you're ready to move forward, pass the two stones over the elemental symbols. As you do, say *[*PET'S NAME*], with the energies of Earth, I am with you in spirit, and you are with me.* Repeat this for each of the elements. When you're done, say *I thank you for being in my life, and for the honor of letting me be in yours. I release you now, but will never forget you.*

Blow out the candle, and keep the stones in your pocket to rub together when you are thinking about your lost pet.

*You can keep it simple and use a bowl of soil, a feather, a tealight, and a cup of water, if you wish.

May 8

Rosemary Spell
for Good Memories

You'll need:
- A bundle of fresh rosemary
- A bundle of fresh lavender
- Blue string or ribbon

The month of May is tied strongly to the Green Man, a folkloric archetype associated with vegetation and new growth. It's also when herb gardens begin to bloom, so if you've planted rosemary and lavender, you can do this working to aid in restoring good memories and emotional healing. Do this spell when you're feeling down, and you need a reminder of the many good experiences you've had.

Hold the rosemary and lavender stems together to form a combined bundle, and use the blue string to wrap one end tightly. As you do, breathe in the fresh scent of the herbs, and think about the good things in your life. Realize that even when things are not going your way, you still have your happy memories to hold on to. Place the herb bundle under your pillow so you can smell it in your sleep, and dream about your many blessings.

May 9

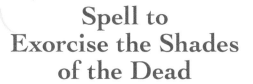

Spell to
Exorcise the Shades
of the Dead

You'll need:
- A bag of dry black beans
- A bronze bowl

May 9 was the festival day of the Roman Lemuria, a feast in which the head of each household performed rituals to send away malevolent spirits. If you think an unhappy spirit is hanging around, do this working to get rid of it. Do this spell outside at night, when it's fully dark.

Stand outside your front door and remove your shoes, holding the beans in the bronze bowl. Walk around your house in a counterclockwise direction, tossing the beans over your shoulder as you travel, saying *With this magic, I send you away. With this magic, I redeem me and mine. With this magic, I redeem my household.* Repeat this incantation nine times as you circle the house. By the time you return to the front door, the bowl should be empty. Stand at the door and bang loudly on the bottom of the bowl, saying nine times *Spirits be gone, shades be gone, ghosts be gone!*

Put on your shoes back, go back inside, and close the door without looking behind you.

May 10

Wooden Spoon
Kitchen Blessing Spell

You'll need:
- Green ribbon
- Fresh basil
- A wooden spoon

The kitchen is the center of the home for many of us, and it's a place where we can make all kinds of magic. From family dinner recipes to spellwork, your kitchen often becomes the spot where people come for comfort, warmth, and sustenance. Do this simple blessing spell in your kitchen to add a bit of mojo into your meal prep.

Use the ribbon to tie the basil to the wooden spoon, and walk in a clockwise direction around your kitchen, beginning at the north wall. As you move, open each cabinet, the refrigerator, and the pantry, waving the spoon like a wand. Point it into each cabinet, and at your stove and oven, saying *Bless this kitchen, hearth and home. Bless this kitchen and the meals prepared. Bless this kitchen and the magic made.*

After you've circled the entire kitchen, hang the spoon near your oven or inside the pantry as a reminder that magic is present.

May 11

Wild Weather Water for Spellwork

You'll need:
- A bowl
- Glass bottles in a variety of colors

May's weather patterns are notoriously unpredict-able, but there is a good chance that at some point you're going to see a storm. Whether it's a light shower on a sunny day or a completely windy blowout with hail, May is full of wet and wild meteorological phenomena. Take advantage of this, and gather some rainwater to use in different types of spellwork.

Place your bowl outside after the rain begins, and store the rainwater in one of your bottles. For spells related to personal empowerment, use water gathered during a windstorm, and store it in a gold or purple bottle. If you want to use water in a working for healing, collect it during a sun shower, and keep it in a blue bottle. For love magic, collect rainwater shaken off rosebushes, and put it in a pink or red bottle. If there is massive thunder and lightning, store this water in a white bottle so you can use it in spells to re-energize yourself, or for cleansing and purification.

May 12

Mother and Child Bonding Spell

You'll need:
- An orange candle
- Two rose quartz stones
- A white lily in a pot

Mother's Day falls annually on the second Sunday in May. If you haven't seen your mom in a while, or if you haven't seen your kids for some time — simply by virtue of geography or other circumstances — do this spell to strengthen the bond between parent and child. If your mother is deceased, this spell can help you reconnect with her in your dreams.

Light the candle, and hold the two stones together in your hands. Think for a moment about the love between you and your mother — or, if you're the parent, consider the love between you and your child. Say *Love and joy, hopes and smiles, connecting us across the miles. Distance does nothing to keep us apart, mother and child, joined at the heart.*

Press the rose quartz stones, side by side, into the soil in the lily pot, and place it in a sunny window as a reminder of the ever-growing love shared between mother and child.

May 13

Braid Spell for a Growing Relationship

You'll need:
- Three strands of red cord or yarn
- Three strands of pink cord or yarn

In many magical traditions, braiding and weaving can come in handy as a spellwork technique. As you twist and tangle strips of material or fibers together, visualize the intent of your spell—it can almost turn into a meditative exercise. One of the most practical uses of braiding magic is to strengthen a growing relationship.

Pair up the pieces of cord evenly so you have three pairs, each containing a red and a pink strand. Hold all six strands together and knot them at one end. Begin braiding the pairs slowly, crossing one set of red and pink over the next. As you do, say *Red for you and pink for me, love grows and grows and grows times three. Pink for me and red for you, love grows strong and fast and true.*

When you've reached the end of the cords, tie a second knot so the braid won't unravel. Hang the braid in your home, or tuck it under your mattress.

May 14

Spell to Leave an Unhappy Relationship

You'll need:
- A photo of you and the other person
- 3 feet of black string or yarn
- Scissors

One of the hardest parts of the end of a relationship is the acknowledgment that it's time to let go. We all have our reasons for sticking around—the kids, the house, financial obligations, a sense that we have failed if we leave—but sometimes we need a little nudge to take that last step. If you know you need to break free of your relationship, do this working to cut the cord.

Fold the photo in half three times, and wrap it completely with the black string, working in all directions so you can no longer see any part of the image. As you wrap the string or yarn, say *Where once was love and two hearts blended, now there is a relationship ended. I wish you no harm and wish you no ill, but I must break free, it is my will.*

Bury the wrapped photo outside for seven days, and use this week as an opportunity to do the mundane things necessary to help you leave. On the final day, dig it up, and use the scissors to gradually cut away the string, saying *I cut the cord, I'm free today, I sever ties and walk away.* Dispose of the cut string and the photo, and begin moving forward with your life.

May 15

Business Communication Spell

You'll need:
- A marker or a felt-tip pen
- Three bay leaves

May 15 was the date of the Mercuralia, a festival honoring the god Mercury in his role as patron of commerce and business. He was also known as the messenger to the gods, and is associated with communication. If you've been waiting for news of a professional nature and it just doesn't seem to be forthcoming, use this spell to give slack communicators a little magical nudge. Do this working on a Wednesday, if possible.

Write the name of the person who's supposed to be contacting you on both sides of the bay leaves, saying *I wait for news I need so much, get to work and get in touch!* Place the bay leaves near whatever medium you hope to deliver the news—if you're waiting for a call, tuck them in your cell phone case. If you're hoping for an email, place them under a corner of your laptop.

May 16

Luscious Lipstick Beauty Spell

You'll need:
- A mirror
- A fresh tube of lipstick in a bold color*
- A bowl of rose petals

Hera was the queen of the gods of Olympus, and was well known for her beauty. Each year on May 16, a festival was held in her honor, which means this is a good day to work on spells that make you feel glamorous and confident. In principle, a glamour spell doesn't change your actual physical appearance, but it does change the way people perceive you. It's a subtle difference, but an important one. The bottom line? Feel beautiful, and other people will see you as gorgeous!

Stand in front of your mirror, and place the lipstick in the bowl of rose petals. Say *Beauty within and outside of me, beauty I feel and what others now see. Luscious color to last a while, on my spirit and on my smile.* Apply the lipstick, blow yourself a kiss in the mirror, and admire how awesome you are. Keep your lipstick handy for touch-up applications as it wears off during the day. When you go to bed at night, keep the lipstick in the bowl of rose petals beside your mirror.

If you don't usually wear lipstick, or you normally prefer a sedate and conservative color, this is your chance to reinvent yourself. Go vibrant and sassy, and see how it makes you feel!

May 17

Hagstone
Fertility Spell

You'll need:
- A green candle
- A hagstone
- A piece of leather cord

I n many cultures, a hagstone—a stone that has a naturally occurring hole all the way through—is used for fertility magic. Depending on what sort of fertility you wish to bring into your life, consider using a hagstone for spellwork. You may want to boost your financial abundance, add blessings to your garden, or increase the size of your family.* Remember, fertility can manifest in a number of ways.

Light the candle, and hold the hagstone between your hands. Concentrate on it, thinking about the sort of fertility and abundance you wish to see growing in your life. Say *Fertility magic in this stone, fertility magic of my own, fertility growing and surrounding me, as I will, so it shall be.* Thread the stone on the leather cord, tie a knot, and wear it as a necklace until your fertility goals have been realized.

If you are someone who struggles with medical issues that cause infertility, keep in mind that this working should be done in addition to, and not in place of, treatment with a qualified professional.

May 18

Spring Wildflower Inspiration Crown

You'll need:
- A selection of wildflowers with stems
- Ribbons in silver, purple, and gold

During the merry month of May, wildflowers are blooming all over the place. Why not take advantage of what's available, weave flowers into a crown, and use it for inspiration when your creative juices are feeling blocked? Find a field where you can collect wildflowers undisturbed, and do this spell on a bright, sunny afternoon.

Gather up as many wildflowers as you can, and find a quiet place to sit. Weave the flowers together into a circle, much like the daisy chains you made as a child, until you have enough to sit comfortably on your head. As you're connecting the flowers, let your mind wander a bit, opening up to the issue at hand—in which aspects of your life do you need to unblock your creativity? Add the ribbons for a finishing touch, and place the crown on your head, saying *Inspiration come to me, vision and creativity, ideas and insight flowing free, as I will, so it shall be.*

Relax in the field, enjoying the fresh air and sunshine, until you are ready to go home. Hang the floral crown over your workspace to help inspire you.

May 19

Journal Spell
to Fight Your Fears

You'll need:
• A blank journal and a red pen

D o you ever wish you had more courage? Sometimes if we could only speak up, take that first step, or make a leap of faith, we'd feel better. A lack of courage isn't something to be ashamed of, and it's certainly something you can overcome with a bit of time and effort. This spell, which will take three weeks, should help you get focused and brave enough to make the decisions you need to.

Begin by making a list of what scares you on the very first page — not the mundane things like spiders or heights, but the big, life-changing issues, like *Being alone* or *Making a new start*. Once you have your list, turn the page. Each day, for the next 21 days, write the list again, but add the words *I am not afraid of…* in front of each item. Speak it out loud as you write it.

After you've written your list on the last day, build a fire, burn the journal, and send away your fears for good.

May 20

Flower Moon Spell for Career Changes

You'll need:
- A copy of your résumé
- Three sprigs of mint

The full moon in May is the Flower Moon — and rightfully so, since gardens are blooming and blossoming all over the place! It's a time of new beginnings, and a great month to work on magic related to careers, jobs, and even your education. If you've considered switching to a new position at your current job, trying a new field altogether, or even going back to school to get your degree, use this spell to help you move on up in the world. Do this spell on a sunny day, right before the full moon.

Fold your resume into a paper airplane, tucking the mint into the folds, and as you do, say *Moving up, toward the skies, my career goals are high. Let others see with open eyes, the work I do, and recognize.* Take the airplane to a place that represents your career goals — like an upper level of your office building or a fancy building on campus — and tuck it where no one can find it. Once you've moved along in your career, go back and retrieve your résumé.

May 21

Gemini Spell to Attract Your Opposite

You'll need:
- A small, flat box, such as a breath mint tin
- A small mirror that will fit inside the box
- A photo of yourself and a photo
of the person to whom you're attracted

They say opposites attract, and if you have your heart set on an individual who is your complete polar opposite, magic might be just what you need to get him or her to notice you as a potential love match. Gemini is the Zodiac symbol that begins on May 21, and although it's typically a sign associated with twins and duality, it's also related to things that are opposites, or mirror images, of one another.

Place the mirror on the bottom of the box, face up, and place the two photos, side by side, looking into the mirror. As you do, say *We're nothing alike, this I know, nothing in common, but love may grow. The opposite of you is reflected in me, as I will, so it shall be.*

Put the lid on the box, and tuck it away under your bed.

May 22

Prosperity Cookie Spell to Get a Raise

You'll need:
• Your favorite cookie recipe and ingredients
• A toothpick

Everyone likes to feel prosperous, and everyone loves cookies, so why not combine the two? Make a batch of cookies to give to the people upon whom your livelihood depends—bosses, coworkers, and even customers.

Prepare the cookies according to the recipe. Before putting them in the oven, use the toothpick to poke a small dollar symbol into the top of each one. As they bake, the holes will close and become barely noticeable. Take the cookies to work, and share with clients, customers, and coworkers—anyone who might be able to help you increase your income!

May 23

Rosewater
Spell to Keep Your
Lover Close

You'll need:
- Honey
- Rosewater*
- A piece of paper and a pen

Roses are beginning to bloom by the end of May, and they're typically associated with love. If you're worried that your lover might have a bit of a wandering eye, you can use magic to sweeten the relationship a bit, and keep him or her from straying.

Mix the honey and rosewater together in a jar. Write your lover's name on the paper nine times. Soak the paper in the honey and rosewater blend for nine days. Once you have done this, keep the jar in a safe place near your bed. Your lover will stay close to you.

To make rosewater, place ½ cup dried rose petals in a container, and add 2 cups hot distilled water. Once the mixture has cooled, strain out the petals, and use the leftover water.

May 24

Broom Spell to Protect an Empty House

You'll need:
- A strip of white cloth
- An old broom

No one likes to leave their home empty for an extended period of time. If you're going on vacation, or if you're in the process of building or buying a home that's sitting unoccupied right now, do this working to protect the site from intruders, vandals, and other mischief-makers.

Tie the cloth around the broom handle, leaving a loop, and thoroughly sweep the front doorway, brushing any dust or dirt outside. As you sweep, say *No one's here, no one's home, all will leave this house alone. Broom in the door both night and day, keep the troublemakers away!*

Use the loop of cloth to hang the broom on the inside doorknob. Close the door, lock it behind you, and know your house will be undisturbed when you return.

May 25

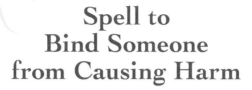

Spell to Bind Someone from Causing Harm

You'll need:
- A photo of the person
- Black ribbon
- A glass jar with a lid

In a number of modern magical traditions, a binding spell is done to prevent someone from causing harm to other people or to themselves. This you can use this simple binding spell to metaphorically tie the hands of the individual who is presenting you or your loved ones with a threat.*

Wrap the photo with the black ribbon, knotting it nine times. As you do, imagine the individual leaving you and your loved ones in peace, and say *You have no power over me, and I bind you from doing harm to me. You have no power over others, and I bind you from doing harm to others.*

Place the wrapped photo in the jar and put on the lid, then bury it on the north side of your home. If the person's behavior improves and you wish to release the binding, simply dig up the jar and unwrap the photo.

If you're concerned that someone in your life may be self-harming, this spell should be used in addition to, not in place of, proper mental health counseling. Likewise, if someone has threatened physical harm to others, be sure to get law enforcement involved as well.

May 26

Honeysuckle Spell to Dream of Love and Passion

You'll need:
- A red candle
- Three honeysuckle branches or vines

Between the onset of spring and midsummer, honeysuckle flowers are typically in bloom. Their strong, sweet scent is associated with passionate love, as well as dreams and intuition. If you want to dream about your lover—real or potential—do this spell at night, right before you go to bed. Try to do it on a Monday if possible.

Light the candle beside your bed, and twist the honeysuckle vines around one another, being careful not to knock the flowers loose. As you do, say *Sweet as honey, below and above, send to me the dreams of love. Show my lover's adoring face, and wrap me up in love's embrace.*

Tuck the honeysuckle beneath your pillow, blow out the candle, and dream of your lover.

May 27

Rabbit Magic Energy Spell

You'll need:
- Brown paint and a paintbrush
- A smooth, flat stone

Rabbits are everywhere in late May, hopping around with seemingly endless amounts of energy. If you're feeling physically drained* and run-down, take advantage of rabbit magic. Make a talisman that will help you give yourself a metaphysical pick-me-up. Do this working at sundown, when rabbits start becoming active.

Paint a rabbit symbol on one side of the stone—it doesn't have to be fancy, but should clearly be a rabbit (think whiskers, floppy ears, and a fluffy tail). As you work, say *Hop and bounce with energy, rabbit magic blessing me. Give me a boost by the waning light, verve and vigor, day and night.*

Carry the stone in your pocket, and when you start feeling worn out, hold it in your hand as a reminder of rabbit energy.

* Be sure to consult your health-care provider to rule out physical causes of fatigue.

May 28

Spell to
Keep a Secret

You'll need:
- A hand mirror
- A bay leaf

Occasionally, we find ourselves in possession of knowledge that we wish we didn't have—either accidentally or because someone told us something we didn't really want to hear. If you're worried you might accidentally blab and betray a confidence, do this working to help you stay strong and keep your mouth shut. Do this spell outside on a windy day, and go where you can be completely alone.

Hold the mirror in one hand so you can see your face, and hold the bay leaf in the other. Say into the mirror *I know something I should not know, I heard something I should not have heard, I learned something I should not have learned.*

Whisper the secret three times to the bay leaf. After the third time, say *I will never speak these words again, never will I betray a friend.* Tear the bay leaf into tiny pieces, and scatter it into the wind, letting go of the secret.

May 29

Spell to Bless a
Freshly Planted Garden

You'll need:
- Milk
- Honey
- Wine
- A bowl

Chances are good that you've planted your garden in the past couple of weeks, so now that your flowers and herbs are getting ready to grow, it's the perfect time to do a bit of blessing magic. May 29 was the date of the Ambarvalia festival, an agricultural holiday in which tributes were made to the gods and goddesses of planting and crops to ensure a bountiful harvest. Do this spell early in the morning, after the sun has risen.

Blend equal parts of milk, honey, and wine in the bowl. Beginning at the north side, walk around your garden in a clockwise direction, dipping your fingers in the mixture and sprinkling it on the soil. As you do, say *Honey for the bees, wine for the Divine, and milk for growth in this garden of mine.*

Pour anything left in the bowl right into the center of your garden.

May 30

A-Maze-Ing Spell to Meet New People

You'll need:
• A picture of a maze and a pencil

Spring is often associated with mazes—their twisty turns and unexpected corners often put us in places we never thought we'd be. You may not have access to a real, full-size maze (although if you do, this spell just got a whole lot easier), so instead use a maze image printed from your computer, or torn from a book of mazes and puzzles.

Start at the beginning of the maze, using the pencil to work your way slowly through. As you move around corners and hit dead ends, start thinking about the kinds of people you would like to draw into your life. Are you looking for love? Do you just want better friends? Consider your options as you move the pencil from beginning to end. By the time you reach the end of the maze, you should have imagined the different types of individuals you hope to meet.

Fold the paper into a small square, and put it in your pocket or your purse next time you go out. You'll attract many of the people you imagined during your journey through the maze.

May 31

Spell to
Honor the Dead

You'll need:
- A photo or memento of the person
who passed away
- A white candle

The last Monday in May is observed as Memorial Day in the United States, and this holiday honors members of the military who died in service to their country. If you have a family member or a friend who perished in service, do this spell on Memorial Day to honor this individual. Try to time this working for sundown.

Place the photo or memento in front of the candle. Light the candle, and say *[NAME], I honor you and I remember you. Your sacrifice is known, and your name is worthy. Brave spirit, courageous soul, fallen warrior. In life and in death, you will not be forgotten.*

Take the time to watch the candle burn, and remember how much the deceased meant to you. Allow the candle to burn out on its own, and when it has done so, place the photo in a position of honor in your home.

June

By June, much of spring's rain and unpredictable weather has drawn to an end. It's when the days get warmer and our gardens begin to bloom in earnest, and it's also the season of the summer solstice. This is a time of powerful sun energy, and we can celebrate the magic of warm days and long hours of light.

At this time of year weddings and love go into high gear, flowers are abundant, herbs pop up everywhere, and the trees are full of fruit and leaves. Spellwork in June focuses on all the magical sun power that makes things grow and flourish, from our garden to our heart and our spirit.

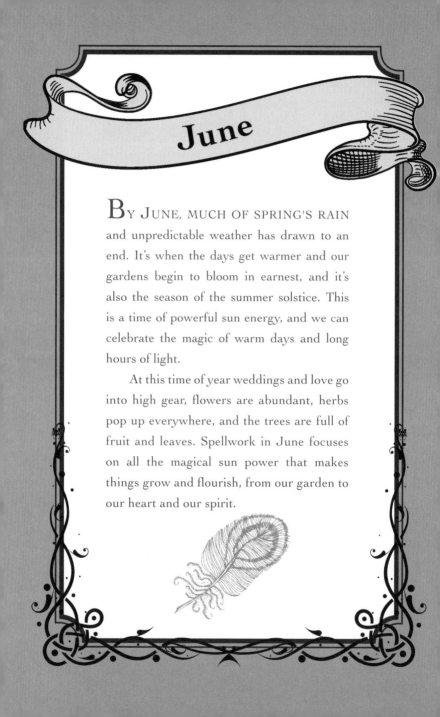

June 1

Spell to Protect
Your House Keys

You'll need:
- A bundle of sage
- Your house key

The first day of June many have observed as the festival day of the goddess Cardea, who is associated with doors, hinges, and locks. This is a good time to do a spell to protect your house keys. If you're forever misplacing them, this working will not only keep them where you can find them easily, it will also add a layer of protection into the lock itself. Do this spell at your front door.

Light the sage, and smudge all around the lock on your front door. If you have a deadbolt, smudge that too. As you do, say *Key to my home, easily found. Key to my home, to me you're bound.*

Pass the key through the sage smoke, then insert it in the lock. Say *Key to lock, lock to key, never stray away from me.*

Remove the key, which will now be much easier to keep track of.

June 2

Strong
Marriage Glove Spell

You'll need:
- A glove worn by you and one worn by your partner
- Gold thread and a sewing needle

June is a month for weddings, so it's no surprise that it's a good time to work on magic related to marriage. If you're already married or in a long-term relationship, this spell can strengthen the bond between you and your partner. If possible, plan this working for a Friday.

Put the gloves together so the thumbs are lined up with one another, the pinkies with each other, and so on. Beginning with the ring fingers, stitch the gloves together, working all the way around the outside of each finger, down along the wrist opening, and back up. As you sew, repeat the words *Hand to hand, heart to heart, strong in love, and never to part.*

When you've finished stitching, store the gloves in the room of your home in which you and your partner spend the most time together.

June 3

Spell to Compel Truthfulness

You'll need:
- 4 ounces grape-seed or jojoba oil
- 1 ounce sandalwood oil
- 1 ounce pure vanilla extract

Think someone might be acting evasive? Brew up a bit of truth oil, and use it to compel this individual to be honest with you. If you regularly encounter people who are less than truthful, you can blend this in advance and keep it on hand for just the right occasion. If you do prepare it ahead of time, be sure to store it in a dark-colored glass bottle.

Blend the oils and extract together by pouring them into a bottle and swirling it gently in a clockwise motion. As you do, say *Truth be told, no more lies. Now it's time for honesty, telling the truth will set you free.*

To use this oil on someone you think may be lying to you, add a small amount to your fingertips, then shake their hand or touch their clothing.

June 4

Spell to Mend a Relationship

You'll need:
- Two blue candles:
one for you and one for the person you hurt
- Dried rosemary

None of us is perfect, and we've all made mistakes. Unfortunately, sometimes those gaffes hurt the people we care about, and we have to work twice as hard to regain their trust. If you've done something to damage a relationship with someone you love, in addition to owning up to your mistakes and apologizing, do this spell to add a little metaphysical mojo into the repair process.

Light the candles, which represent healing. Take a few moments to think about the lapses you've made in the relationship, and realize it's time for you to own them. Say *I was wrong and I am sorry. I have broken your trust and I wish to regain it. I ask your forgiveness so we can move forward.*

Rub the rosemary between your palms, releasing its oils, and say *I have brought deceit to this relationship. From now on, it starts anew, and I bring nothing but honesty and love.* Sprinkle the crushed rosemary around the candles, and let them burn out on their own. Once they have, sweep up the rosemary, and scatter it outside your front door. Make an effort to do all the mundane things you must in order to salvage the relationship.

June 5

Sacred Stone
Divination Spell

You'll need:
- Nine flat, smooth stones of similar size
- Silver paint and a paintbrush
- A drawstring pouch large enough to hold all the stones

In some folklore, the summer months are deeply connected to cairns and stone circles. You can bring this aspect of the warmer months into your life by using stones as a method of divination for just about any question at hand.

Place the stones in front of you, and paint each with a different symbol or word, as follows: YES, NO, EARTH, AIR, FIRE, WATER, SUN, MOON, and SPIRIT (or SELF). Once the paint has dried, place all nine stones in the bag. Close your eyes, and think about the question at hand. Reach into the bag, and withdraw a stone. Think about how the answer applies to your situation.

YES and NO are self-explanatory. EARTH represents family and the security of the home. AIR symbolizes wishes and dreams. For FIRE, consider passion and outside influences, while WATER represents healing and cleansing. If the answer to your question relates to power and energy, you may see the SUN stone appear, and the MOON stone is tied to intuition and wisdom. Finally, the SPIRIT/SELF stone indicates that the answer to your dilemma can be found within you, and is tied to the choices you make for yourself.

If a single stone doesn't tell you what you need to know, draw three stones instead, and see how the answers relate to each other.

June 6

Summer Herb Dream Vision Spell

You'll need:
- A muslin bag
- Any three of the following: bay leaves, ash tree leaves, dried holly, mugwort, mint
- A journal and a pen

Summer is the season in which our herb gardens begin blooming in earnest, and many herbs are associated with dreams and visions. By placing a collection of these magical plants under your pillow at night, you'll increase your chances for prophetic dreams. Use dried or fresh leaves and plants in this working.

Fill the bag with equal amounts of the herbs you've selected, and as you do, say *Dreams and visions in my sleep, knowledge will be mine to keep, tell me what I need to know, as I rest, it shall be so.* Place the bag under your pillow at bedtime. Use the journal to jot down any dreams you have in the night. Do this as soon as you wake up so the information is still fresh, and take time later to evaluate the meaning.

June 7

Fire Spell
Hospitality Blessing

You'll need:
- A white candle
- A fireproof bowl or dish

The Vestalia was a festival held in ancient Rome, beginning each year on June 7, in honor of the goddess Vesta. A deity of the home and all things domestic, Vesta is associated with hearth fires and hospitality. In her honor, you can use fire today to bless the dwelling for all who enter it. Do this working at sundown, sitting by a window on the west side of your home.

Light the candle, and place it in the bowl. Hold up the bowl to the window, so you can see the candle flame and the setting sun. Say *Fire warm us, fire guide us, fire light our way. Happy home, happy hearth, hospitality is here to stay.*

Stay by the window until the sun has set, and extinguish the candle.

June 8

Stay With Me Spell

You will need:
- A pair of your own underwear,
  and a pair of your lover's
- 3 yards of red cord
- Nine cinnamon sticks

Ever feel like your love relationship may be on its last legs? In addition to doing all the mundane things necessary to salvage it, sometimes a bit of magic can give you the extra time to make things right again. If you're worried your lover might be on the way out the door, do this working to help you try to recover what was lost.

Wrap the two pair of underwear—ideally worn recently—around the cinnamon sticks. As you do, visualize yourself and the one you love together and happy again. Wrap the red cord around the underwear bundle as many times as you can. As you are wrapping, again picture yourself and your lover back in a satisfying and healthy relationship. Once you have used all the red cord, tie it off in a knot.

Keep the bundle under your pillow or your bed as long as you wish the love to last, and be sure to work on nonmagical things to repair the relationship. If you decide later that it's better to move on, unwrap the cord and separate the underwear.

June 9

Wildflower Spell to Heal from Heartache

You'll need:
• A blue candle
• A bunch of wildflowers with stems

Wildflowers are abundant in many areas during June, and if you're coping with the pain of heartache after a divorce or an ugly breakup, this spell can help with the healing process. If possible, do it on a sunny afternoon and collect the wildflowers yourself. In addition to the magical benefits, this gives your spirit the added value of the peace provided by walking outdoors.

Light the candle, and begin slowly weaving the wildflower stems together into a long garland. You can braid or twist them, or even tie them in a way that forms a flower chain. As you do this, say *My heart was broken, but the pain does not define me. My soul was wounded, but the hurt will not stop me. My spirit was damaged, but the ache does not limit me. I have loved and lost, and now I will live again.*

Once you've connected all the flowers, join the ends so they make a circle. Blow out the candle, and place your healing wildflower ring around it. Leave it in place for the next seven days. When the time is up, return the flowers to the field in which you picked them, say *good-bye*, and walk away without looking back.

June 10

Eye-Opening Spell

You'll need:
- A photo of the person you want to help
- A black marker
- A photo of the person who is causing trouble

Ever get frustrated with someone in your life who refuses to see others for what they really are? Sometimes people refuse to see the truth, no matter how much you try to show them. Use this working to help open the eyes of a friend or a loved one who could use a little more awareness about someone who may be causing dissent.

On the picture of the person you wish to help, draw an open eye in each corner. As you do, say *Eyes wide open, no longer closed, see this person for whom they truly are.*

Place the two photos right sides together, so the eye symbols are facing the image of the person who is causing problems. Say *No more blinders, no more blocks, no more boundaries, see this person for whom they truly are.*

Put the two photos, still together and facing each other, under something heavy until the individual you're helping is illuminated about the character of the other person.

June 11

Coffee Spell to Change Your Luck

You'll need:
- A cup of unused coffee grounds
- A clean washcloth
- A green ribbon

It's frustrating when you're having a run of bad luck, especially if it seems like nothing will ever get better. Don't worry: Sometimes the universe just needs a little kick in the pants to get things back on the right track. Do this working to change your own fortune.

Place the coffee grounds in the washcloth to form a bundle, and twist the corners together. Tie the bundle shut with the ribbon. When you shower, use the coffee bundle to scrub your skin from head to toe. As you do, say (or sing, if you enjoy a jaunty tune), *Bad luck goes on down the drain, washing all bad luck away. Plenty of room for good luck on me, good luck is all I plan to see.*

Once you've scrubbed your entire body, stay in the shower until you see the last of the coffee grounds disappear down the drain, taking your bad luck away with them.

June 12

Moonstone Spell for Wisdom and Guidance

You'll need:
- A moonstone ring or pendant, or a loose stone
- A bowl of water

J une's birthstone is the moonstone, and it is considered sacred in many cultures. Many believe the moon-stone allows those who wear it the gift of prophecy, and it's also closely tied to matters of wisdom. If you feel like you need a bit of help when it comes to wise decision-making, or in issues that require you to know what lies ahead, use this moonstone spell to give you a little extra guidance. Try to time this spell for the week before the full moon, and do it at night when the moon is visible.

Position the bowl so the moonlight is reflected in the water, and place the moonstone inside. Put your hands on the side of the bowl, look up at the night sky, and say *Wisdom, I need you. Guidance, I call to you. Perception, I welcome you.*

Allow the moonstone to sit overnight in the water, under the full moon. In the morning, put on the ring or pendant—if it's a loose stone, carry it in your pocket—and allow the moon's wisdom to guide you as you go about your day.

June 13

Shoe
Protection Spell

You'll need:
- Your favorite pair of walking or running shoes
- A black permanent marker

This season, before it gets too hot, is a great time of year to go outdoors and get in some exercise, and that could mean you'll spend a lot of time on your feet. If you're a hiker, backpacker, jogger, or if you just try to get in a few laps around the neighborhood, do this spell on your shoes to protect you as you travel.

Flip over the shoes, and on the bottom of the left one, write the word SAFE. On the right, write SOUND. Put the shoes on, and sit on the floor, knees bent and to the side, so the soles touch each other. Say *I may walk the world round, but I'll always come home safe and sound. I walk for miles both far and near, hale and hearty when I return here.*

Wear your shoes when you go walking or running, and be sure to check the soles periodically to see if you need to refresh the words.

June 14

Sun Spell to Light Your Way

You'll need:
• A gold candle

Have ever been outside in the dark in the middle of the night, when the moon and stars weren't out to illuminate your path? It can be pretty frightening to stumble around with no idea where you're headed. Sometimes we get lost emotionally or mentally, and that's when a bit of metaphysical light can come in handy. In June, we have the longest days of the year as the summer solstice approaches, so it is a perfect time for this spell. Start this working just before sunrise — you may have to get up pretty early to do it.

Sit outside, facing east, and light the candle. Make sure you're in a location where you'll have a clear view of the sun as it breaks over the horizon. As you wait for the sun to come up, say *I have wandered off my path, I have walked blindly in the darkness. Now I am ready to see where I am headed. I am ready for new journeys and new directions. I am ready to follow the sun and welcome the light.*

Repeat this as the sun comes up, and when the sun has risen enough to shine directly on you, extinguish the candle and be glad the daylight is back in your life.

June 15

Father and Child Bonding Spell

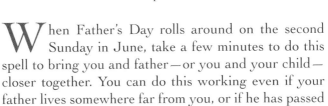

You'll need:
- A red candle   • Gold string
- Two sticks, one to represent the father and one to represent the child

When Father's Day rolls around on the second Sunday in June, take a few minutes to do this spell to bring you and father—or you and your child—closer together. You can do this working even if your father lives somewhere far from you, or if he has passed away. Try to do this spell outside on a sunny morning.

Light the candle, and close your eyes for a moment. Think about how important the bond of father and child is. Hold one of the sticks in each hand, and raise them up to the sun, saying *Mighty sun, bringing life and light to us all. I honor you today, and honor the sacred masculine energy of fatherhood. I celebrate the men in my life, who raised me, who love me, and that I myself am raising.*

Bring the sticks together, and use the string to wrap them together firmly. As you do, think about all the men who have made a difference in your life—and if you're a father, consider how your actions and words impact the children you have brought into the world. When you're done, extinguish the candle, and keep the sticks in a place where you can see them each day.

June 16

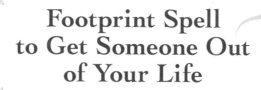

Footprint Spell to Get Someone Out of Your Life

You'll need:
- Sea salt
- Cayenne pepper or dried habanero flakes
- Sulfur powder

Want to get someone out of your life who has been causing trouble? Some magical traditions use footprints as a link to the individual. You can do a bit of spellwork if you know where the person has walked.

Blend equal parts of the three ingredients in a bowl until they are well mixed. Go outside to a place the person has walked, such as a doorstep or sidewalk. Sprinkle the mixture on the ground, walking backward so you don't step in it. As you do, say *[NAME], stay away, [NAME], get out of here, [NAME], you are unwelcome.*

The person will no longer feel comfortable walking where you've sprinkled the powder, and will learn to stay away.

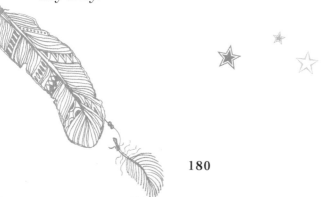

June 17

Strong Sun Moon
Spell to Sweeten
Someone's Disposition

You'll need:
- A photo of the individual
- A brown paper lunch-size bag
- A cup of sugar

June's full moon is known as the Strong Sun moon, for obvious reasons. Falling right around the summer solstice, this full moon is associated with bonding with our friends and family, as well as nurturing our gardens and souls. You can also work on nurturing your relationships if someone in your life is a bit of a sourpuss. Use this spell to sweeten his or her disposition a bit. Do this working on the night of the full moon.

Place the photo in the bag, and pour the sugar in slowly. As you do, say *Sweeten your life, sweeten your world. Take joy in all that life has to offer, and share your joy with others.*

Dig a hole under a tree or bush, and bury the bag, sugar and all. The person's mood and demeanor should improve substantially.

June 18

Wrench Spell to Adjust Your Own Attitude

You'll need:
- A blue candle
- A photo of yourself
- A small wrench

None of us like to recognize that we're being negative or cranky, but we all are at one time or another. It's hard to admit, but sometimes we need an attitude adjustment. And what's a great tool with which to make adjustments? A wrench! You probably have one in your home, but if you don't, borrow one from a friend. When your mood improves, you'll be glad you did.

Light the candle, and wrap the photo of yourself around the wrench's handle. Hold it firmly in your dominant hand, and say *An attitude adjustment is what I need, changing toward the positive in word and deed. Negative thoughts are going away, tighten up my attitude beginning today.*

Drip some of the melted candle wax on the edge of the photo to seal it around the wrench. Extinguish the candle, and place the wrench in a spot where you'll see it regularly as a reminder that you're making adjustments.

June 19

Luggage Protection Spell for Air Travelers

You'll need:
- Rosemary oil
- A hematite stone
- Your luggage tag

Got a trip on a plane planned this summer? Use this simple spell to make sure your luggage gets to the proper destination safely. Do one for each bag or suitcase that you're checking at the airport, especially if you have to change planes along the way. The energy of the sun can serve as a perfect magical booster. Do this working outside on a sunny day.

Pour the oil into a bowl and add the hematite stone. Hold the bowl in your hands and raise it up to the sun, saying *Watch over my belongings as I travel, protect me as I fly. May we arrive together safely, protect us in the sky.*

Dip your finger in the oil in the oil, and use it to draw an image of the sun on the back of your luggage tag to protect your bags in flight.

June 20

Summer Solstice Power Spell

You'll need:
- Gold or yellow paper
- A purple pen or marker
- String

The summer solstice, also called Litha or Midsummer, falls around June 20 each year, although the date can vary. This is the longest day of the year, and in many magical traditions, it's when the sun is most powerful. Full of blazing, masculine energy, the sun is a source of warmth and life. Why not spend some time outside enjoying it, and boost your own personal power levels? Do this spell at noon, when the sun is at the highest point in the sky.

Cut three equal-size circles from the gold paper; the easiest way is to trace a cup or a small plate. On each of the circles, use the purple marker to trace a spiral from the center to the outer edge. Take your time as you do this, saying *Power growing in the sky, power growing within me, power growing overhead, power growing strong times three.*

On each of the circles, draw your spiral a little faster than on the previous one. When you've finished the third circle, hold all three up to the sun. Say *Power of the sun, revitalize me, strengthen me, and make me grow!*

Poke holes in the circles, and use the string to connect them. Hang them in a sunny window as a reminder of your own empowerment.

June 21

Cancer the Crab Spell for Social Success

You'll need:
- Rose oil
- A glass of saltwater
- A dried bay leaf

June 21 is the first day of the Zodiac sign of Cancer the crab, which is a water sign. Cancer is associated with both sensitivity and social skills, so if you occasionally feel awkward around other people, this working can help you overcome that. If you have access to saltwater straight from the ocean, use it; if you don't, make your own by combining sea salt with spring water.

Put three drops of the rose oil into the saltwater, then crumble the bay leaf and add it in. Stir the blend in a clockwise direction, and as you do, say *Confidence and power, energy of the sea, I am self-assured and poised, and people listen to me.*

Before you enter a social situation in which you'll be expected to speak, anoint your wrists and throat with a bit of the water.

June 22

Midnight Sun
Fortune-Telling Magic

You'll need:
• A bonfire
• Any of the following herbs:
sage, mugwort, heliotrope, tobacco leaf
• A journal and a pen

In some areas, particularly those in far northern latitudes, June 22 is celebrated as the day of the midnight sun. It's the point in the year when there are twenty-four hours of light, and in a lot of magical traditions this makes it a perfect day to do a bit of magical fortune-telling. You may not live in a place that's illuminated all day long, but around the time of the summer solstice, you're getting plenty of sunlight, so do a bit of divination in the hour right before full darkness descends.

As the sun sets beyond the horizon, light your bonfire. Take a moment to get a good blaze going, then toss the herbs into the fire. Close your eyes, and breathe in the fragrance of the herbs, all of which are associated with divination. Focus on the questions you have about the future, then open your eyes and look at the flames. What do you see? Shapes? Patterns? Figures of people or animals? Write down what you observe so you can remember it later. Once you feel like you're no longer seeing anything new, allow the fire to go out on its own. Take some time to think about what you've seen, and how those images relate to your question.

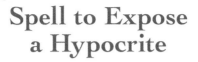

June 23

Spell to Expose
a Hypocrite

You'll need:
- A knife
- A black candle
- A box of whole cloves

Got someone in your life whose hypocritical words and actions are causing strife? Why not use magic to expose the person's true nature? This simple working will make the individual show his or her colors, and will end the problematic behavior.

Use the knife to inscribe the person's name on the candle, then poke the cloves into the wax, making sure you puncture through the individual's name. As you do, say *I banish your duplicity, your false pretenses, and your two-facedness. The truth is exposed, your hypocrisy will be known, and your words can do no more harm.*

Light the candle, and let it burn all the way down. Once it's finished, leave what's left in the person's yard. If he or she lives far from you, take it away from your home for disposal.

June 24

Anxiety Relief Bath Spell

You'll need:
- A blue candle
- Sandalwood oil
- A cloth pouch containing equal parts
St. John's wort, lavender, and chamomile

If you're feeling a bit anxious, a relaxing bath can help relieve your stress. In addition to mundane measures—like eliminating the cause of your anxiety or taking prescribed medications—try this bath spell to help alleviate your symptoms.

Light the candle, and begin running a warm bath. Add seven drops of the oil, and hang the pouch over the faucet so the water runs over it. Once the tub is full, climb in and close your eyes. Imagine your anxiety and worries leaving your body through your pores. As you wash, picture yourself scrubbing away what has caused you stress. When the water has cooled, get out of the tub and let the water drain. As it does, say *I am calm, I am cool, I am collected. Anxiety does not rule me, fear does not guide me, stress does not defeat me.* Once the tub has drained, allow yourself to air-dry without a towel, and extinguish the candle.

June 25

Incense Spell to Banish Negativity

You'll need:
- Bay leaves, dried rosemary, and sandalwood
- A bowl
- Charcoal disk for burning incense

The summer solstice was just a few days ago, and the nights are already beginning to lengthen. It may not seem like much right now, but in a few months it will be getting dark early. As we gradually move into the darker half of the year, it never hurts to be proactive. Get a jump on banishing any negative influences in your life with this simple incense spell. Do this during the waning phase of the moon.

Mix equal parts of all three herbs in a bowl. Use the charcoal disk to burn this loose blend at night near an open window. When you light it, say *Darkness be gone, ill will be gone, disharmony be gone, floating away into the night.*

Repeat this for seven nights.

June 26

Beach Magic to Overcome Obstacles

You'll need:
• A sandy beach with waves
• A stick

The beach can be magical indeed—ask any worn-out parent who finally gets a chance to relax in the sand for an hour or two! It tends to transform us, and it's a place where all the elements come together: sandy earth, warm breezes, blazing sun, and cool water. If you have planned a beach vacation for the summer, use the natural energy of the shore to overcome obstacles that may be in your path. Do this spell at sunset.

Go to the beach as the sun is setting, and take off your shoes. Find a quiet spot away from everyone else, and begin to count the waves. When you get to nine, stand in the wet sand where the waves break. Use the stick to write in the sand the obstacles you wish to overcome. For example, you can write FEAR, SELF-DOUBT, or ANGER. As the waves wash over the word or words you've written, imagine those obstacles being swept out to sea. When the tide has erased the words completely, leave the beach and don't look back.

June 27

Firefly Divination to Find Lost Items

You'll need:
- A firefly
- A clean jar

By midsummer, fireflies are typically all over the place. Some people believe, for obvious reasons, they can lead you when you've lost your way. However, if you're willing to trust your intuition a bit, they can also help you find lost items. If you're outside as the sun goes down, capture a firefly in a jar to help locate things you've misplaced in your home.

Catch a firefly—or two or three—in the jar and take it into your house. Say *Lead me, guide me, light my way, help find the thing I've lost today.* Release the firefly, and follow it to see which room it goes into. Once you enter the room, watch to see where the firefly goes next—chances are good it will lead you straight to the missing item. However, if you get a sudden flash of inspiration, don't discount it—remember to trust your instincts!

June 28

Spell to Stop a Wrongdoer

You'll need:
- A red marker
- A photo of the person
- A roll of electrical tape

Got someone in your life causing trouble who just won't back off because he or she never seems to get caught in the act? Maybe it's the neighborhood hoodlum, a class bully, or someone at work who thrives on dissent. If you know an individual who always manages to get away with shenanigans because he or she is flying under everyone else's radar, now is a good time to put a stop to things once and for all.

Write the word STOP! across the photo of the person causing trouble. Crumple the photo, and wrap it with the entire roll of electrical tape, forming a ball. Take the ball far from your home, and throw it as hard as you can. As it's in the air, flying away from you, wave good-bye and tell it farewell. Turn around and walk away before it hits the ground, and don't look back to see where it landed.

June 29

Spell to Draw
New Customers

You'll need:
- A green candle
- Dried chamomile
- A dollar bill

Whether you own a big business, work for someone else, or simply run a small hobby industry on your own, customers are the lifeblood of your profit. Without them, finding success can be a challenge. Use this spell to draw new customers into your business, and reap the rewards!

Light the candle, and wrap the chamomile into the dollar bill, folding it into a neat packet so none of the loose herbs fall out. As you do, say *Business boom and business grow, customers come and money flow*.

Place the folded dollar bill under the cash register at your place of business—or, if you work virtually, under your laptop. Replace it every seven days until customer traffic picks up.

193

June 30

Moonflower
Dream
Travel Spell

You'll need:
• Three moonflowers, freshly picked

The moonflower, which is part of the same family as the morning glory, is a vining blossom that gets its name because it opens at night. Moonflowers have a heady, fragrant scent, and in some traditions they are used in shamanic rituals. While you should never ingest them—they are toxic to consume—you can use the fragrance to inspire dream journeying.

Place the moonflowers under your pillow right before you go to bed. As you do, say *Moonflower for my journey's guide, in my sleep, no secrets hide.* When you lie down and close your eyes, think about where you'd like to go in your dreams, and inhale the intoxicating scent of the moonflowers.

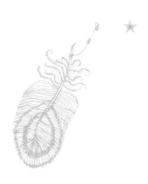

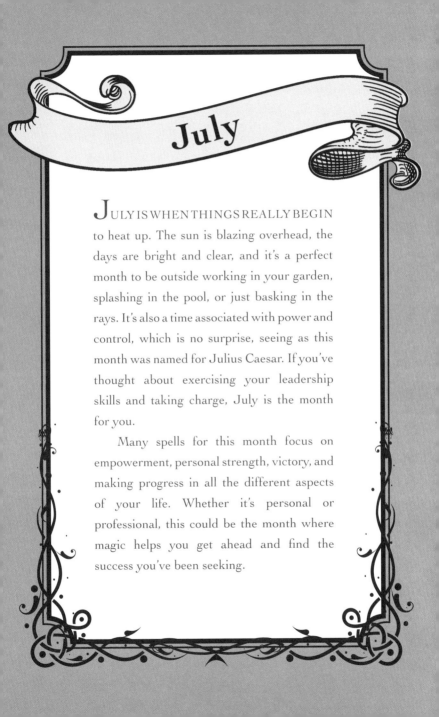

July

JULY IS WHEN THINGS REALLY BEGIN to heat up. The sun is blazing overhead, the days are bright and clear, and it's a perfect month to be outside working in your garden, splashing in the pool, or just basking in the rays. It's also a time associated with power and control, which is no surprise, seeing as this month was named for Julius Caesar. If you've thought about exercising your leadership skills and taking charge, July is the month for you.

Many spells for this month focus on empowerment, personal strength, victory, and making progress in all the different aspects of your life. Whether it's personal or professional, this could be the month where magic helps you get ahead and find the success you've been seeking.

July 1

Spell for Charitable Causes

You'll need:
- Laurel leaves
- A business card, photo, or other item representing your charity
- A purple cloth bag

In some agricultural societies, the beginning of July was a time in which green corn was set aside for planting the following year. Ideally, this meant that if someone had been struggling, or suffered blight on their crops, the rest of the community could help by contributing their own corn for planting. That way, everyone worked together for the common good and made sure no one went hungry from one year to the next. If you're involved with charity work in your own community, do this spell—preferably on a Sunday—to help bring aid to your cause.

Rub the laurel leaves on the business card or item you've chosen to symbolize the charity. As you do, say *Success and accomplishment to this worthy cause, helping hands and helping hearts. Awareness and growth never to pause, if everyone does their parts.*

Tuck the leaves and the business card in the bag, and bury it on your own property, or in a place near the charity's offices.

July 2

Honey Spell to End a Quarrel

You'll need:
- A lemon
- Honey
- A blue cloth

We've all quarreled with other people, but when the argument is with someone you love or care about, it is even worse. To compound things, if you're both stubborn, you can quickly find yourselves at an impasse. Do this spell to end an ongoing disagreement with a friend or family member so you can both move on and rebuild the relationship.

Slice the lemon in half. One part represents you, and the other part symbolizes the other person. Spread honey on the half designated to be yours, and put the lemon back together so the honey is sandwiched between the halves. Say *What was sour now is sweet, what was broken now is joined, what was damaged now is repaired.*

Wrap the lemon in the blue cloth, and bury it near your front door.

197

July 3

Seashell Spell for Better Listening Skills

You'll need:
- An orange candle
- A large unbroken seashell

Remember when you were a child, and you held a seashell to your ear to hear the roar of the ocean? If you're lucky enough to go to the beach this summer—or even if you have shells you collected on past visits—use a bit of seashell magic to improve your listening skills. Do this spell in the evening, after dark.

Light the candle, and raise the shell to your ear, using your dominant hand. Listen to the sounds of the waves as you watch the candle's flame. Say *I will listen to more than words, I will hear more than sounds. Heeding both what's said and what is not, as clarity abounds.*

Blow out the candle and keep the seashell in a place where you can see it, as a reminder of your pledge to be a better listener.

July 4

A Spell for Liberty and Independence

You'll need:
- Three pieces of ribbon in red, white, and blue

The July 4 holiday is when many of us take a few extra minutes to think about the importance of liberty and independence. While you probably don't need to go quite as far as America's founding fathers did to achieve your own liberation, if you do need to break away from things or people that make you feel undervalued or unequal, this is a perfect day to do it.

Go someplace outdoors where you can work undisturbed, and sit quietly for a while. Think about what's holding you back, and who or what is restraining your independence. Knot the three ribbons together on one end, and slowly begin braiding them together. As you do so, say *I am free, I am independent, and nothing will hold me back. I am free, I am independent, and I make my own choices. I am free, I am independent, and I claim my liberty.*

Once you've finished braiding the ribbons, dig a small hole and bury them. Go home and start making the mundane changes in your life that will help you break free.

July 5

Spell to Find a New Lover

You'll need:
- A ring, bracelet, or other piece of jewelry
- A blooming rosebush
- A cup

If you're feeling lonely and need a new lover—or if you're just ready to replace your existing partner—do this spell on a sunny summer day to draw a new lover to you. It does involve a bit of sacrifice, though, as you'll have to give up a piece of jewelry.

Bury the jewelry in the soil beneath the rosebush. As you do, say I *raise this rosebush with tenderness and care, drawing love my way.* Each day, repeat this as you tend the rosebush to make it bloom healthy and beautiful. When you see a bee land on one of the roses, carefully catch it in the cup. Whisper to the bee *Find the lover that's right for me, and send them my way.*

Release the bee, so it can fly off and find a lover for you.

July 6

Basil Magic to Keep Your Lover Faithful

You'll need:
• Thirteen basil leaves

No matter how low-maintenance you may be, odds are good that you demand a couple of things from the people you love: honesty, for example, or faithfulness. If you'd like to add a little magical mojo into your love life to keep someone loyal, do this working in early July, when the basil plants are blooming with reckless abandon.

Dry out the basil leaves in your oven by placing them on a baking sheet, at 200°F for 20 minutes, and then allowing them to dry for 12 to 15 hours.

Once they've cooled, rub them between your palms until they crumble easily. Sprinkle the crumbs on the bed where you and your lover sleep, especially around the spot where their heart would be when they lie down, and under your partner's pillow. Your lover's heart and mind will remain true to you.

July 7

Blessing Basket Spell for Summer Weddings

You'll need:
- An empty basket
- Symbols of romance—hearts, chocolates, wine, candles, and so on
- Pink and red ribbons

In the ancient world, July 7 was the day of the annual festival of Adonia, which honored sacred weddings. If you have friends getting married this summer, use this simple spell to put together a basket of blessings for them.

Fill the basket with the items you've chosen to represent the couple's love. As you place each one, say *Two hearts now become one, blessings to both, love growing stronger as the each day passes by. I give you my blessings, that your love may bloom, growing stronger as the years go by.*

Tie the ribbons around the basket's handle, and give it to the couple as a wedding gift.

July 8

Sun Spell
for Leadership

You'll need:
- A gold marker or gold paint
  and a paintbrush
- Three oak leaves

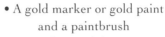

The sun is a powerful source of energy. It's the giver of life and the bringer of warmth, and it is often associated with power and success. In the past, it was even connected to the right of divine kingship. If you're outside on a bright, sunny day, use that natural warmth and energy to boost your own leadership skills. Try to pick the leaves straight from the tree, rather than gathering those that have already fallen.

At noon, sit outside under an oak tree, when the sun is high above you. Write or paint on the leaves the qualities that you believe important to a good leader. You might choose WISDOM, FAIRNESS, STRENGTH, or INTEGRITY. Whatever you select, once you've written them, place the leaves together in a stack and fold them three times. Hold the folded leaves between your hands, saying *I will lead by example, by my actions, and with my heart. I will hone my skills, listen to feedback, accept criticism gracefully, and be someone that others can look up to. I am a leader in my heart.*

Unfold the leaves, and tuck all three of them into the bark of the tree so your skills can grow and strengthen as the oak tree does.

July 9

Spell for Protection on the Water

You'll need:
- A gold coin
- A piece of hemp rope

July is one of the most popular months for boating. After all, the sun is out, the water is warm, and if you're lucky enough to have access to watercraft, it's the perfect time of year to get out and enjoy the day. During the seafaring heyday of centuries past, sailors believed that gold served as a protective element during voyages. Some of them wore gold earrings to keep them safe from falling overboard, since at that time most people couldn't swim. Use a bit of gold to protect your boat and its passengers.

After all the passengers get on the boat, but before casting off, use the rope to secure the coin to the bow side of the mast, making sure the coin is complete covered. As you wrap the rope around the mast and the coin, say *Protection for this boat, keeping it worthy. Protection for the passengers, keeping us safe. Protection for all, that we may return home again.*

Even after coming back to land, leave the coin in place to keep your vessel safe in your absence.

July 10

Harvest Home Guardian Spell

You'll need:
- Brush, twigs, and weeds from your garden
- Sturdy twine

In parts of Europe, July 10 is the celebration of a legendary being called Knut the Harvester. This reaper-like figure is a representation of the harvest, and parades are held in which giant wicker figures are displayed to ward off evil spirits. After you've pulled weeds and overgrowth from your garden, use what you've gathered to create a home guardian for the summer harvest season.

Gather up the brush, twigs, and weeds and shape them into an approximation of a human figure (it doesn't have to be large). Wrap the twine around the legs, arms, and head to keep everything together. As you wrap the twine, say *Watch over my home in the time of reaping, watch over my house in the time of gathering. Watch over my garden in the time of ending, watch over my crops as the earth begins dying.*

Place your guardian figure near the door, or in a place where it can oversee your garden.

July 11

Lemon Pie
Love Strengthening
Spell

You'll need:
- Your favorite lemon meringue pie
  recipe and ingredients
- Raspberries

It's often said the way to your lover's heart is through his or her stomach, and if you enjoy cooking, you should be very lucky in love indeed! Lemons are a bright, sunny fruit associated with love of the purest sort. Use your favorite lemon meringue pie recipe with a few delicious seasonal raspberries to sweeten the magic and strengthen your existing love match.

Prepare the pie according to the recipe, but before you add the meringue topping, use the raspberries to create a heart shape on top of the pie. As you do, say *Sweet as can be, you and me. Love is true, for me and you.*

Add the meringue topping, and bake the pie. Once it has cooled, serve it to your lover to sweeten the relationship.

July 12

Pennyroyal Spell to Deter Thieves

You'll need:
- Several pennyroyal stems

Pennyroyal is a popular herb in a number of magical traditions, and it has a wide variety of uses, mostly connected to strength and protection. In the past, it's been used for everything from keeping sailors safe on the high seas to protecting pets—and their owners—from fleas. It even comes in handy for warding off the "evil eye" in some European belief systems. You can use this member of the mint family to protect your home and property from thieves and vandals.

Braid together the pennyroyal stems to create a long garland. As you wind them in and out of each other, say *Pennyroyal protect my home from those who would cross my threshold. Pennyroyal protect my home from those who would covet my belongings. Pennyroyal protect my home from those who would cause destruction and damage.*

Once you've braided all the stems together, hang the garland over your front door, on the outside, to keep burglars and other troublemakers away.

July 13

Spell to
Eliminate Self-Doubt

You'll need:
- A mirror
- A piece of paper and a pen

It's perfectly normal to experience occasional feelings of self-doubt; at some point we all do so. Unfortunately, sometimes this behavior can lead to self-sabotaging behavior, and it becomes a vicious cycle. Kick this bad habit to the curb with a simple spell to help you stop second-guessing yourself and eliminate self-doubt from your life.

Stand in front of the mirror and begin writing a letter to yourself—not the self that you see in the mirror, but the self that tells you to question every decision. Address this internal you, and explain why that voice is just plain wrong. You can say things like *I am smart and make good choices*, or *I look at all my options before moving forward*. Once you're done, sign the letter *My true self*.

Look in the mirror, and read the letter aloud three times. When you're done, say *No more doubt, no more questions, no more misgivings. It's time for me to move and get back to living*. Tear the letter into as many pieces as you can. To dispose of it, either dig a hole somewhere away from your property and bury the pieces, or toss them into a moving body of water to carry them away.

July 14

Feverfew
Healing Magic

You'll need:
- Equal parts dried feverfew, rosemary, and juniper berries
- A cloth drawstring bag

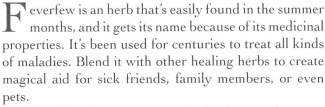

Feverfew is an herb that's easily found in the summer months, and it gets its name because of its medicinal properties. It's been used for centuries to treat all kinds of maladies. Blend it with other healing herbs to create magical aid for sick friends, family members, or even pets.

Blend the herbs together in the bag, and as you do, say *May [NAME] be healed, and maladies vanish. May [NAME] be well, and sickness leave. May [NAME] be whole, and illness flee.*

Pull the drawstring tight. Place the bag under the sick person's pillow, or on a windowsill in the room in which he or she is resting.

July 15

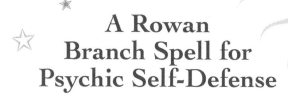

A Rowan Branch Spell for Psychic Self-Defense

You'll need:
- Five rowan twigs
- Five sage branches
- Yellow thread

The rowan tree is associated with protection magic — especially when it comes to self-defense of the metaphysical variety. If you think someone is messing with your head psychically, this simple charm can help keep your entire family's problems at bay.

Pair the rowan twigs and the sage branches together, so you've got five sets, each containing rowan and sage. Cross the pairs over each other to form a star, and use the thread to bind them together at the points. As you do this, say *Five points to form a magic star, five points wherever we are, five points to defend us near and far.*

Close your eyes, and imagine the light of the stars enveloping you, forming a protective barrier around you and the other members of your household. Hang the star on the front door to keep negative psychic energies out.

July 16

Queen Anne's Lace Spell for Fertility

You'll need:
- A green candle
- Calendula oil
- Dried Queen Anne's lace flowers

Fertility magic is one of the oldest documented uses of herbal spellwork. If you're hoping to conceive, in addition to ruling out possible medical issues that might impede fertility, do this spell in the middle of July, when Queen Anne's lace is abundant. Try to time this working for a Thursday, during the most fertile part of your monthly cycle, preferably in the week before the full moon.

Before lighting the candle, apply a thin coating of oil along the entire length of it, starting at the top of the candle, and rubbing down to the middle. Next, move to the base and rub the oil back toward the middle, ending where your first coating of oil left off. Once you've done that, roll the oiled candle in the dried Queen Anne's lace, and as you do, say *Tonight I am fertile, like the earth. I am ripe, like the orchards. I am abundant, like the meadows. Fertility come to me this night, as the moon becomes full.*

Light the candle, close your eyes, and imagine your body full and luscious, like the moon above. Allow the candle to burn out on its own.

July 17

Blessing
Moon Magic

You'll need:
- Spring water in a cup
- Hyssop leaves

July's full moon is known as the Blessing Moon—and no wonder, because this time of year the fields and gardens are full and abundant, and a reminder of just how fortunate we are. This is a good time to do magic in which we try to make time for relaxation, as well as develop our hobbies, skills, and other interests. This spell can help you focus on the blessings of new endeavors. Do this working outside, after the full moon has appeared in the sky.

Hold the cup of water up to the moon, and close your eyes. Think about the blessings you have in your life, and how fortunate you are to be able to start new things. Once you've relaxed, crush the hyssop leaves into the water, and say *I am blessed, I am fortunate, I have abundance in my life. New adventures begin, a new me steps forward. I count my blessings, I count my good fortune, I count my abundance.*

Begin counting off the blessings in your life, such as *I am blessed to have my health, I am blessed to have my children, I am blessed that I love my career,* and so on. When you've finished, offer the cup to the moon once more, and pour the hyssop water on the ground at your feet.

July 18

Chamomile Magic for Good Fortune

You'll need:
- 4 quarts water
- 2 cups chamomile flowers
- Clear glass jar with lid

Chamomile is typically blooming during the hot summer months, and it's an herb associated with good luck and fortune, especially in gambling or games of chance. In a number of folk magic traditions, it's believed that washing your hands in chamomile water will increase your opportunities for good luck in your endeavors, whatever they may be. If possible, pick the chamomile first thing in the morning, while the dew is still fresh.

Bring the water to a boil, and add the chamomile. Reduce the heat and allow it to simmer for 20 to 30 minutes. Strain out the flowers, and allow the water to cool. Store it in the glass jar, and when you need to increase your luck, wash your hands with the water. As you do, say *Good luck, strong luck, fortune come my way. Good luck, strong luck, fortune all day.*

July 19

Ruby Spell to Attract Love

You'll need:
- A pink candle
- Red rose petals
- A ruby

The birthstone for July is the ruby, and its bright red color makes it perfect for a bit of love magic, especially if you've been single for a while and are feeling alone. Use a ruby to help bring some summer love your way.

Light the candle, and think about all your lovable qualities. What is it about you that romantic partners find attractive? Scatter the rose petals around the candle, enumerating your merits aloud, like *I am loyal, I am confident, I am honest, I am spontaneous.*

After you've scattered the rose petals, hold the ruby over your heart, and close your eyes. Say *I draw love my way, into my life. Someone will be worthy, and I will know when they arrive.*

Imagine the ruby drawing love to you like a magnet. Extinguish the candle, and keep the ruby in your pocket, or —better yet —as a necklace close to your heart.

July 20

Tomato Spell to Remove Negative Influences

You'll need:
- A black candle
- Nine ripe tomatoes

Tomatoes are everywhere in July, so why not use them for a bit of magic? In many traditions of spellwork, they are used in place of apples and are associated with healing, love, and the elimination of harmful influences. If you have someone in your life pushing you or a family member to make bad choices, tomatoes are going to come in very handy indeed.

Stand just outside your front door, and light the candle. Say *Harmful influences, negative control, I block you from our lives.*

Walk around the house in a counterclockwise direction, placing a tomato on the ground at each corner on all four sides of the house, saying *No more influence, no more control, I block you from our lives.* This should leave you with one tomato by the time you return to the front door. When you get there, place the tomato on the ground near the corner of the doorway, on the side opposite the hinges. Say *We make our own choices, we make our own decisions, you have no more power.*

Go inside and close the door behind you. As the tomatoes decompose on their own, the person's influence will wane as well.

215

July 21

Egg Divination to
See if Luck is Coming

You'll need:
- A fresh egg
- A glass of cold water

Pythagoras was a well-known mathematician in the ancient world. In fact, he was so famous that we still use his theorem today. However, many people are unaware of the existence of his daughter Damo, who was not only a philosopher but also a seer. Venerated on July 21, Damo's gifts of prophecy were honored long after her death. Today is perfect for doing some divination of your own.

Crack the egg and separate it, putting aside the yolk. Drop the white into the glass of water. If it sinks to the bottom, you'll have good fortune in the coming year, but if it floats on the surface, you may find yourself facing some challenges.

July 22

Ocean Spell for Cleansing the Soul

You'll need:
• A glass jar with a lid

July 22 was sacred to Neptune, the god of the sea. Since this is when when many people visit the beach, it is also a perfect time to do a bit of spiritual cleansing in the ocean. After all, the sea contains not only salt, which is associated with purification, but also moving water, which can carry metaphysical baggage far away from you. Do this spell at sunrise, or as close to low tide as possible. If you can, time it for the week after the full moon.

Stand barefoot in the sand, along the waterline. Close your eyes, and consider all the things that are weighing you down. What aspects of your life are draining you of your spirit? These things need to go away. Imagine these issues trickling slowly out of your body, from your head down to your toes. Let the water wash over your feet, and as the tide ebbs and flows, picture it drawing your problems away with it, carrying them far out to sea.

When you feel refreshed, as though the ocean has cleansed your soul, slowly count to nine, then fill your glass jar with water. Take the water home with you, and if you need a bit of a boost later, drizzle the water over your toes in the bathtub, and send your problems down the drain.

July 23

Leo Spell for Bravery

You'll need:
- A red candle
- A piece of parchment and a red pen

The Zodiac sign of Leo the lion begins on July 23, and this symbol has long been associated with courage, stoutheartedness, and bravery. If you're about to jump into a situation that makes you fearful, do this spell before you get going. It will give you a little confidence boost, and help you be brave in the face of things that frighten you.

Light the candle, and say *I am brave and strong, like the lion in my heart. I am brave and strong, like the lion in my soul. I am brave and strong, like the lion that I am.* Draw an image of a lion on the parchment. It doesn't have to be fancy; it just needs to look like a lion to you. Once you've made your lion, draw a protective circle all the way around it. Fold the parchment and place it in your shoe. As you put on your shoe, say *I walk with courage, I walk with bravery, I walk with pride, and I fear nothing.*

Extinguish the candle and go face your fears.

July 24

Peppermint Purification Spray

You'll need:
- A large clear glass jar or pitcher filled with water
- Several handfuls of peppermint leaves
- A spray bottle

If you've ever seen mint growing in a garden, you know it has absolutely no boundaries—it will merrily creep through fences and out of pots. Fortunately, mint is a very useful herb, especially in purification magic. The mint family includes a variety of different plants, from peppermint and spearmint to comfrey and catnip. Use peppermint or any of its relatives to do a bit of household purification for the summer months, especially on hot days when you're trapped inside.

Place the glass jar out in the sunshine first thing in the morning, and add the peppermint leaves. Allow it to steep in the sun all day, then transfer the water to the spray bottle. On days when everyone's a bit cranky and sweaty and stuck indoors, spritz it around the house to purify the air and the spirit, saying *Fresh and clean, minty green. Rejuvenate from here to there, it's time for us to clear the air.*

Renew as the need arises.

July 25

Spell to Help
You Be More Patient

You'll need:

- A blue candle
- Lavender, fresh or dried

Ever find yourself getting impatient with other people? Waiting for others to get stuff done, or make decisions, can be agonizing. Unfortunately, when we show our impatience and annoyance, it can cause problems. This means that often the best course of action is to develop a bit of compassion and understanding, and to cultivate patience. It's hard to do, but with a bit of magic, you can make it work.

Light the candle, and watch the flame for a few minutes. Think about the things that other people do that frustrate you, and recognize that in addition to them changing their behaviors, you need to alter your own response. Imagine your annoyance being replaced with the healing energy of the candle. Cup the lavender in your hands, and take a deep breath, inhaling its calming aroma. Say *I am at peace, I am relaxed, I will be patient,* three times.

Extinguish the candle, and sprinkle the lavender around your home. When you find that someone is getting on your nerves and making you impatient, repeat the mantra above, and remember the quieting scent of the lavender in your hands.

July 26

Horseshoe
Protection Magic

You'll need:
- A horseshoe
- Yellow ribbon
- Iron nails and a hammer

July 26 is the day on which a festival was observed honoring Sleipnir, the magical eight-legged horse that Odin rode. Horseshoes are associated with good luck, but in many cultures they're also connected to protection magic. For luck, a horseshoe is usually hung with the open end up, but for protection, it's typically displayed with the open end facing downward. If possible, use a horseshoe that has actually been worn.

Wrap the horseshoe in the yellow ribbon, winding it from end to the other until the entire thing is hidden. As you wrap the ribbon, say *Protection from harm, protection from ill will, protection from any strife. Horseshoe hanging on the wall, protection in my life.*

Use the iron nails to mount the horseshoe to the wall outside your front door to protect your home and everyone in it.

July 27

Sage Wand Magic

You'll need:
- Fresh sage branches
- Fresh rosemary branches
- White cotton thread

Plenty of metaphysical traditions use sage, which is associated with cleansing and purification. While you can buy sage wands in a number of places, many people believe making your own allows you to imbue them with your own magical energy, which makes them even more powerful. If you make your own sage smudge wands, you can use them to cleanse your home when you need to.

Bundle the sage and rosemary together, and use the thread to wrap them snugly. As you bind the thread around the herbs, say *Cleansing and clearing, by my hand. Purification and protection, by my spirit. Smudging and strengthening, by my will.*

Once you've bound the herbs together, tie a loop in the thread to hang the bundle to dry. Use it later to smudge your home in purification spells.

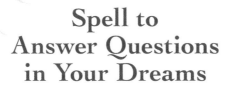

July 28

Spell to
Answer Questions
in Your Dreams

You'll need:
- A piece of silver paper and a pen
- Mugwort

The human mind is vast and complicated, and our dreams can tell us a lot about ourselves. Sometimes they tell us what we already know, but refused to acknowledge. If you've been struggling with a question, do this spell to find the answer in your dreams. Do this working right before you go to bed.

Write your question on the paper, and fold it securely around the mugwort. Tuck the paper and the herbs inside your pillowcase when you go to bed. As you drift off to sleep, breathing the smell of the mugwort, clear your mind of everything other than the question at hand. The answer should come to you in your dreams, so you'll know how to proceed in the morning.

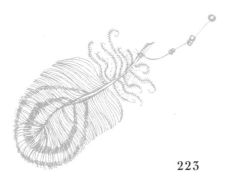

July 29

Guardians of the Garden Spell

You'll need:
- Four stones of similar size and shape
- Acrylic paints and paintbrushes

In addition to household guardians, many cultures call upon protective beings to watch over the fields and crops, especially as the harvest season approaches. Whether you have a large farm or just a few herbs in pots on your apartment steps, you can do this working to ensure that the guardians will be keeping an eye on your harvest.

Paint the stones in colors that correspond to the four elements—brown or green for earth, white or silver to symbolize air, red or orange for fire, and blue to represent water. After the paint has dried, place the stones in your garden so earth is to the north, air to the east, fire in the south, and water at the west. As you cite each one, say *Powers of [*ELEMENT*], watch over my garden from the [*DIRECTION*]. Protect my land and the crops in the soil. Protect those who gather the harvest, as we offer thanks and gratitude.*

Keep an eye on the stones as the harvest season begins. If they fall over or get covered in weeds or dirt, tidy them up as they watch over your garden.

July 30

Car
Protection Wash

You'll need:
• Any three of the following:
basil, bay leaves, dill, fennel, parsley, rosemary
• A bucket of hot water
• A brush and sponge

Summer is here, and that means on a bright, warm day, it's a good idea to do a bit of mojo on your vehicle. To protect your car—and those who travel in it—from accidents, mix up a bucket of protection wash and scrub the entire thing. Do this on a sunny afternoon, preferably in the week after the full moon.

Add equal parts of your three herbs to the water, and use the brush to stir them in, moving in a clockwise direction. Wash the entire car with the herb water, paying special attention to the nose of the car and the tires. As you scrub off dirt and grime, say *Safe travels on the road, safe journeys wherever I go. Protection for plastic, rubber and steel, from hood to trunk, from roof to wheels.*

After you've washed the entire car, pour out the water at the edge of your property. Allow the car to dry on its own.

July 31

Garlic Spell to Ensure Good Health

You'll need:
- A head of garlic
- A quartz crystal
- A pot of soil

In addition to protection magic, garlic is well known for its healthful properties, and in the middle of summer there is plenty of it growing. Do this simple spell on a sunny morning, preferably on Sunday, to ensure continued good health and prevent illness from ruining your summer adventures.

Slice the top off the head of garlic so the tops of the cloves are exposed. Hold it cupped in your hands, saying *Warmth and power of the day, good health with me shall stay. Wellness and healthy energy, as I will, so it shall be.*

Press the crystal into the soil, and use your fingers to make a small hole. Plant the garlic head with the open ends of the cloves facing up toward the sun, then cover it with soil. Say *As the sun warms the soil, and crystal magic flows, health and wellness stay with me, as this little garlic grows.*

Add a bit of water to the soil, and place the pot in a sunny place, where the garlic can grow and flourish.

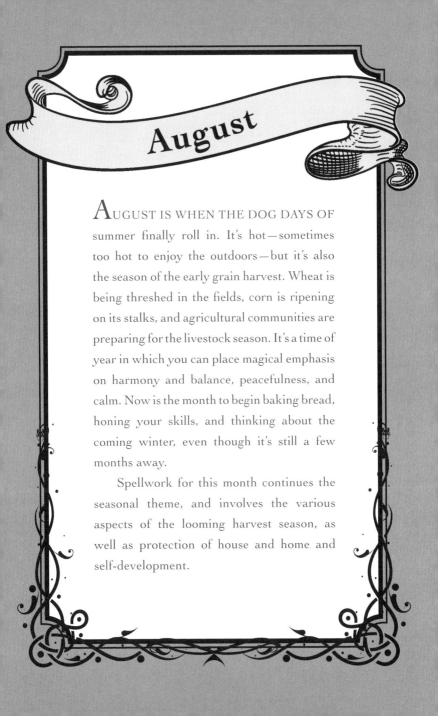

August

AUGUST IS WHEN THE DOG DAYS OF summer finally roll in. It's hot—sometimes too hot to enjoy the outdoors—but it's also the season of the early grain harvest. Wheat is being threshed in the fields, corn is ripening on its stalks, and agricultural communities are preparing for the livestock season. It's a time of year in which you can place magical emphasis on harmony and balance, peacefulness, and calm. Now is the month to begin baking bread, honing your skills, and thinking about the coming winter, even though it's still a few months away.

Spellwork for this month continues the seasonal theme, and involves the various aspects of the looming harvest season, as well as protection of house and home and self-development.

August 1

Bread Baking
Spell for Abundance

You'll need:
- Your favorite bread recipe and ingredients
- A pastry brush
- Melted butter

The first day of August is celebrated as Lammas, which is the modern translation of the Old English phrase *hlaf-maesse*, which means loaf mass. As the grain is harvested, bread is baked and blessed, and there's a sense that home and hospitality is of crucial importance. Grain has become associated with the concept of life, death, and rebirth, and bread itself represents the harvested grain being baked so it can feed our families. Bread ties in perfectly with magic for good health and abundance.

Prepare your bread according to the recipe. Before you place it in the oven, dip the brush in the melted butter and paint the word ABUNDANCE along the top of the loaf. Bake as directed and allow your bread to cool. As you slice it up, say *Abundance for you, and abundance for me. Abundance times two, abundance times three. Slice it up and share it around, blessings for everyone shall be found.*

Serve it with your dinner that night, and know that abundance and blessings are heading toward your family.

August 2

The T-Shirt of
First Impressions Spell

You'll need:
- A plain T-shirt
- Fabric paint and a paintbrush

They say first impressions are important, and often long-lasting, so if you want people to think of you in a certain way, it doesn't hurt to make a good first impression. Believe it or not, it's easy to influence people's perceptions of you simply by presenting yourself in the way you wish to be seen. Combine this with a bit of magical artwork, and you've got a recipe for a positive first impression. Although this spell is designed with a T-shirt in mind, you could adapt it to any other article of clothing, such as a tie or a baseball cap.

First, think about the impression you want to make on other people. Do you wish to present COURAGEOUS, or AWESOME, or BEAUTIFUL? Next, consider a design that represents that aspect of yourself—perhaps a rose for beauty or a lion for courage. Use the paint to create the image on the T-shirt, and as you do, focus on the quality you want other people to see, saying *I am awesome [or sassy, or intelligent, etc.] and people know it, I am awesome and I know it, I am awesome and I'm proud of it.*

Wear your shirt when you go out to a new social situation—and don't tell others what your design means. Let them draw their own first impressions!

August 3

Healing Herb Wreath Spell

You'll need:
- Healing herbs, such as lady's mantle, borage, rosemary, lavender, or peppermint
- A plain grapevine wreath
- Florist's wire and blue ribbon

If you've been growing herbs this summer, now is a perfect time to start harvesting them. Most herbs have some sort of magical correspondence, so you can easily make a bit of magic in your home by gathering the ones you need. Even better, they make everything smell amazing! Here's how you can create a simple healing herb wreath to hang on your door or walls.

Arrange the herbs on the wreath and use the florist's wire to anchor them in place. As you do, visualize healing energy coming from the herbs and working its way through your entire home. Picture health and wellness enveloping everyone who lives there, as well as any guests who stop by. Add the blue ribbon, and hang the wreath on your front door to welcome all who enter.

August 4

Hazelwood Charm to Protect Against Accidents

You'll need:
- Two hazel twigs of similar size
- Yellow thread

The magical folklore of the hazel tree is found in a number of cultures. Branches are often used to make wands and staffs, and the nuts can be used in love magic, divination, and rituals related to wisdom. Hazel is also associated with protection, and you can make a simple charm to carry with you to keep you safe from accidents.

Cross the twigs to form an X, and use the yellow thread to wrap them together, back and forth, where they cross. As you do, say *Magic of the hazel tree, wrapped up in this charm, keep me safe from injury, keep me safe from harm.*

Carry the twigs with you in your purse, hang them on your rearview mirror, or even attach them to your bike for extra safety.

August 5

Spell to
Keep Ghosts Away

You'll need:
- Your favorite incense
- A plate of bread
- Sea salt

In many parts of Asia, August is said to be a time when angry, hungry ghosts roam the world of humankind. They may be disgruntled for a variety of reasons: perhaps they didn't receive an appropriate burial, or their families have dishonored their memory in some way. The month is full of magic designed to keep cranky spirits away, including the lighting of incense, which they seem to like, and the offering of food. Do this spell before dark — it's believed that once the sun goes down, the grumpy ghosts come out in full force.

Stand outside in front of your door, light the incense, and place it in the ground, saying *Angry ghosts, spirits, and haunts, this is not the place for you.* Place the bowl of bread beside it, and say *I leave this offering so that you may walk away quietly.*

Scatter the sea salt on the front step, along the entrance to your home. Say *Angry ghosts, spirits and haunts, it is time for you to move on from this realm, and leave us in peace.*

Step inside, and close the door. Don't open it again until sunrise the next morning.

August 6

Hedge Apple Spell to Keep Spiders Away

You'll need:
• One hedge apple for each door in your home
• A knife

Spiders are active in summer, and while they serve a valuable purpose, like keeping other insects away, if you have an allergy to spider bites—or if you're just afraid of spiders—it's a good idea to keep them out of your home. Hedge apples, also called Osage oranges, can come in handy to create a magical barrier, once they start blooming in your area.

Begin at your front door, and slice a hedge apple in half. Place it on the floor just inside the doorway, and say *Spiders keep outside, spiders go away, outdoors is where you belong, and that is where you'll stay.*

Repeat this at each doorway to your home to keep spiders from entering.

August 7

Wheat Spell
to Draw Money

You'll need:
- Hemp string or raffia
- Nine stalks of wheat

This is the month of the early grain harvest, and crops such as wheat, barley, and corn are traditionally associated with abundance and profit. Hanging wheat stalks in your home can help draw money into your life.

Use the string or raffia to bind the wheat stalks together at the bottom, the middle, and just below the grain pods. As you tie them, say *Wheat abundance from the field, in my life, money yield. Wheat abundance come to me, as I will, so it shall be.*

Leave enough raffia or string to create a loop at the top. Hang the wheat stalks on the front door. If any of the grains fall off, gather them up and put them in your wallet.

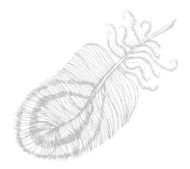

August 8

Corn Meal Spell
to Fight Hunger

You'll need:
- A black candle
- Three ears of corn

The people of Ghana observe the Homowo festival in August each year. This celebration marks the return of the rains to the land in late summer, which allows the crops to grow. Homowo is a time in which people scoff at hunger and famine, and give thanks by offering libations to their ancestors and the gods of the fields. If there are people in your community who don't have enough to eat, in addition to contributing to food drives, you can work this spell to inspire others to help fight hunger. Try to do this on a Thursday, which is associated with generosity.

Light the candle, and say *Hunger, I banish you. Famine, I banish you. Deprivation, I banish you.*

Place the ears of corn so they form a triangle around the candle, saying *May those who are hungry have food to eat, may those who need sustenance find abundance on their plates, may those in need be recognized and helped.*

Allow the candle to burn out on its own, and make a commitment to do what you can on a mundane level to help eradicate hunger in your own community.

August 9

Spell for
Sports Victory

You'll need:
- A gold candle
- Bergamot oil

Mid-August was the time of the original Olympic games in ancient Greece. The finest athletes competed against each other, and victory in sport meant gaining the favor of the gods. If you have a favorite team, or even an individual athlete, facing a tough challenge, do this spell to help tip the odds in their favor.

A photo or logo to represent the team or athlete

Lightly coat the candle in the bergamot oil, then place the photo or logo beneath it. Light the candle, saying *Victory and triumph come, defeat banished forever. I call for victory for this team, and success in this endeavor.*

Let the candle burn out on its own, and go cheer on your favorite.

August 10

Spell to Keep
from Getting Lost

You'll need:
- A yellow candle
- Rosemary oil
- A compass

Summer is a great time to get out and do some exploring while you seek out new adventures. However, if you're in an unfamiliar place, you may occasionally find yourself turned around and unsure of the way back. In addition to using basic common sense, you can do this spell before you begin your journey, whether it's on foot or by car, to make sure you can get yourself home.

Sit in your favorite spot in your home, and light the candle, saying *This beacon I light, to bring me home, this candle I'll find, wherever I roam.*

Dip your finger in the rosemary oil, and use it to write the number of your house on the back of the compass. Hold the compass up to the light of the candle, and say *No matter where I go, no matter what I see, this compass always brings me home, to where I'm supposed to be.*

Extinguish the candle, put the compass in your pocket, and go explore a new place.

August 11

Spell to Speed Along an Insurance Claim

You'll need:
- A copy of your insurance claim
- Three hickory leaves
- A purple cloth

Do you have an insurance claim pending? Outcomes can be tricky to navigate, and even if you're being patient, sometimes it takes a good long while for the end result. To speed success along, do this spell on a Wednesday night.

Fold the insurance claim three times, saying *Favorable decisions come my way, let justice and right prevail.* Tuck the hickory leaves inside the folded paper, and wrap them in the cloth. Tie a knot in the top so the paper and leaves won't slip out, saying *Fair and objective, let this decision be made in my favor.*

Put the entire packet in your filing cabinet, desk drawer, or wherever you keep important papers, and keep it there until the decision has been made.

August 12

Myrrh Spell
to Boost the Spirit

You'll need:
- A small piece of white cotton cloth or muslin
- A blue candle
- Myrrh oil

The first few weeks of August are associated with the goddess Isis, who is a deity of mystery and magic. In ancient Egypt, scented oils were used in rituals for many magical purposes. You can use myrrh oil to give your spirits a lift if you've been feeling down lately. Do this spell outdoors at sunrise.

Light the candle, and close your eyes. Take a moment to think about what's been dragging down your spirits, and realize it's time for you to heal and move on. Put a small amount of the oil on the cloth, and say *Like the sun above me, my spirit rises, my spirit lifts, my spirit soars. May the light of the sun bring me joy today.*

Extinguish the candle, and tuck the cloth in your pocket so you can smell the aroma of myrrh as you go about your day.

August 13

Home Stability Spell

You'll need:
- Sea salt
- Dried lavender, basil, and sage
- A broom, a bucket of water, and a mop

As summer begins to wind down, it's a good time to start thinking about matters of protection magic and of the stability of the home. Do this working as part of your routine cleaning, if there's been disharmony lately, or if you feel like your house needs an added layer of metaphysical security.

Sprinkle the salt on the floor where you're about to clean, then sweep it out the door, and as you do, say *Sweep away unhappiness, purify this home, sweep away the negative, protect this happy home.*

Add the herbs to the bucket of water, and use it to mop the floors, saying *Wash away unhappiness, purify this home, wash away the negative, protect this happy home.* Once you're done, take the dirty mop water outside, to the edge of your property, and pour it into a ditch or a storm drain so it can be carried away.

August 14

Corn Moon Spell
for Spiritual Storage

You'll need:
- A white candle
- Dried corn
- An empty glass jar with lid

A ugust's full moon is known as the Corn Moon, and it's a time of year associated with the harvest. In particular, this season often focuses on storing things away. This is a perfect time to focus on spiritual and physical health, and to harvest what you can to put aside for when you truly need it. Are there sacrifices can you make today that will benefit you further down the road? Do this spell to metaphysically store things for later.

Light the candle, and think about all the blessings and abundance you have in your life. Hold the corn in your hands, and add the kernels to the jar, a few at a time. As you do, count off the good things they represent to you: *joy, good health, spiritual well-being, success*, and the like. Once you've added all the corn, put the lid on the jar. Say *I store these blessings for later, I save this fortune for later, I will embrace this harvest later.*

Extinguish the candle, and put the jar someplace safe. If you're feeling down or disappointed later in the season, pull it out and count your blessings again.

August 15

Apple
Love Divination

You'll need:
- An apple
- A vegetable peeler

Pomona was an ancient goddess associated with the abundance of the fruit orchards. In particular, she watched over the apple harvest, and her festival fell annually in the middle of August. Next time you buy apples, or if you're able to pick your own, set one aside for some divination to see who your future lover may be.

Begin at the stem, and start peeling the apple in one long, continuous piece, saying *Name the lover who's coming to me, show me a letter, that I may see.* Once the piece breaks off the apple, allow it to fall to the floor. What letter does it form? This should give you a hint as to the identity of a future romantic partner.

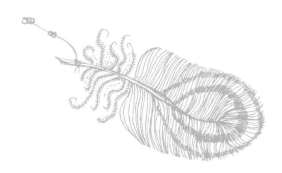

August 16

Grief
Healing Spell

You'll need:
- Three blue balloons filled with helium
- White paint and a paintbrush

Grief is a strange thing, and people express it in different ways. Some may demonstrate their sorrow outwardly, while others tend to internalize it. Regardless of how you react to feelings of grief, part of the process is accepting the need to heal and move forward. When you do this is up to you, but many of us can't function properly until we have given ourselves permission to let go.

Take your balloons someplace outdoors where you can work without disruption. Paint the balloons with symbols of the person or thing for which you're grieving. For example, if it's a person, paint his or her name. If it's a lost love, paint a heart. Once you've decorated all three balloons, hold the strings in your hand and close your eyes. Say *Grief and sadness, I have felt you. Grief and sadness, I have embraced you. Grief and sadness, I release you.*

Let go of the balloons and watch them rise into the sky, carrying your grief away with them. While you may never forget the way you felt, you can now move ahead with the rest of your life.

August 17

Spell to
Pass a Test

You'll need:
- A cup of hot Earl Grey tea
- Your textbooks or notes for the subject
- A grapefruit

In Norse mythology, Odin spent nine days hanging from Yggdrasil, the great tree. When he came back down, he had been granted the gift of vast knowledge. August 17 is the day in which his ordeal is celebrated, so if you have a test coming up, this is a good time to give yourself a magical advantage. In addition to studying and getting a decent amount of sleep the night before, do this spell the morning of a test.

Sip the tea slowly, and as you do, think about all the things you've learned in the subject in which you're about to test. Leaf through the textbook or your notes as a refresher, paying extra attention to concepts or ideas that are still unclear. When you've consumed half the tea, peel the grapefruit and separate it, eating one wedge at a time. Continue perusing your study materials, and when you've eaten all the grapefruit, rub the peels on the front and back covers of your textbook or notes, saying *Knowledge stay with me, learning stay with me, wisdom stay with me.*

Finish drinking your tea, gather up your materials, and go pass your test.

August 18

Offering Spell to the Spirits of the Home

You'll need:
- A green candle
- A piece of freshly baked bread

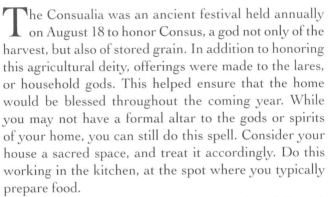

The Consualia was an ancient festival held annually on August 18 to honor Consus, a god not only of the harvest, but also of stored grain. In addition to honoring this agricultural deity, offerings were made to the lares, or household gods. This helped ensure that the home would be blessed throughout the coming year. While you may not have a formal altar to the gods or spirits of your home, you can still do this spell. Consider your house a sacred space, and treat it accordingly. Do this working in the kitchen, at the spot where you typically prepare food.

Light the candle and say *Spirits of my household, I ask you to watch over us. Keep all who live here prosperous and well.*

Place the bread in front of the candle, saying *I offer you bread, this gift from my hearth, as a token of my gratitude.*

Take a moment to think about the blessings your home has received in the past, and the ones you'd like to see in the coming year, and extinguish the candle.

August 19

Spell to Make
Your Dreams Take Flight

You'll need:

• A purple marker
• A kite with plenty of string

August 19 is National Aviation Day in the United States, which celebrates not only aviation accomplishments, but also the birthday of Orville Wright. He and his brother achieved something amazing, which no one believed possible, when they got their plane off the ground. This is a perfect day to do a spell to help your dreams take flight, no matter how far-off they may seem.

Find a large field or open area that gives you plenty of room in which to work. Cover the kite in words that represent your dream. You can use START MY OWN BUSINESS, GO BACK TO SCHOOL, or BUY MY HOBBY FARM. Repeat the words until you've written all over the kite. Launch the kite into the air, and watch as it begins to catch the breeze. As you hold the string, say *My dreams are mine, on this kite. My dreams are attainable, and now take flight. My dreams are magic, and part of me. As I will, so it shall be.*

Release the end of the string, or cut it if necessary, and let the kite fly away, taking your dreams up into the air. While it's still in sight, turn around and go home to get started on the mundane things you need to do to achieve your goals.

August 20

Spell to
Find a Love Match

You'll need:
- A pink candle
- Rosewater
- Two magnets

If you've been dating and you're starting to wonder if the right person is out there, relax. The individual does exist, but he or she may not yet know that you do. Do this working on a Friday to help find your love match.

Light the candle, and dab a bit of rosewater on the outside of each magnet. Hold one magnet in each hand, and say *A love match in my life is what I lack. Positive and negative, opposites attract. Love come in and find a way, my heart is open, I'm ready today.*

Join the magnets together firmly so they don't separate. Extinguish the candle, and carry the magnets in your pocket until you've found your match.

August 21

Peridot Spell to
Gain Professional Respect

You'll need:
- A purple candle
- A peridot stone mounted in a piece of jewelry

There are few things that will suck the joy out of your career like knowing you're not being taken seriously. Whether people are interrupting you in presentations, second-guessing your decisions, or just being disrespectful and rude, it can create a toxic work environment. In addition to doing the mundane things to earn respect—because it is earned—you can also give yourself a bit of a magical pick-me-up to inspire others to treat you the way you'd like them to. Use a peridot stone, which is the birthstone for August, mounted in a ring, necklace, or earrings. Do this spell right before you go to work.

Light the candle, and hold the peridot jewelry in your dominant hand. Say *Working together as part of a team, my coworkers hold me in high esteem. I've earned respect and honor too, this stone with power I imbue.*

Extinguish the candle, and put on the jewelry. Go to work, treat people with dignity, and watch for them to respond in kind.

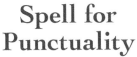

August 22

Spell for Puntuality

You'll need:
- A digital watch
- A quartz crystal

We all know that person who is never on time for anything. Sometimes a bit of a magical nudge is in order to help ensure punctuality. You can do this spell on someone else's behalf, or if that person is you, do this working to help get yourself places on time so that you no longer keep others waiting.

Hold the watch in your dominant hand, and the crystal in the other. Say *Minutes and hours, no more running late, I'll get places on time, and not tempt fate.* Bring the crystal and watch together in your hands, and say *Hours and minutes, I'll be on time, from now on punctual, the choice is mine.*

Wear the watch on the wrist of your nondominant hand, and carry the crystal in your pocket as a reminder that you need to get moving.

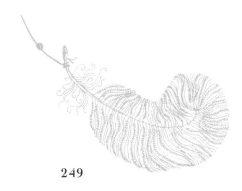

August 23

Virgo Spell
for Earth Energy

You'll need:
• A bowl of clean soil

On August 23, the zodiac sign of Virgo begins. This sign is often associated with the element of earth, and it's a good time to take advantage of the natural energy of the land to boost your own energy levels. Do this spell first thing in the morning somewhere outside.

Sit in the grass, holding the bowl of soil, so you can feel the earth beneath you. Close your eyes and imagine the energy of the land flowing up into your body. Allow it to revitalize you as you relax. Plunge your fingers into the soil, saying *Sun up high and earth below, energy into me will flow. Earth below and sun up high, my energy soaring from land to sky.*

Scatter the soil around you in a circle, working clockwise, and go enjoy the day.

August 24

Spell to Honor
Your Family Ties

You'll need:

• White ribbon

Summer is a time for family gatherings and get-togethers, especially cookouts. Why not enjoy the sunny weather and do a spell to strengthen your family connections? Plan a big feast, invite your loved ones over, and celebrate the magic of clan and kinship. Keep in mind this doesn't have to include only blood family; it can also involve people you consider family of the heart.

After you've eaten, ask all your family members to stand in a circle, with their dominant hands extended to meet each other in the middle. Take the white ribbon, and begin wrapping it loosely around each person's wrist, joining them to the next. As you do, say *Kin and clan, family ties, we celebrate the love that binds. From each of us our strength we take, our family tree bends but never breaks.*

Once everyone's wrists are wrapped, add your own into the family circle, and loop the remaining ribbon over the joined hands. Take a moment to reflect on how fortunate you are to have people who love you, and that you may love in return.

August 25

Bath Spell for Transition and Change

You'll need:
- Peppermint leaves and bay leaves
- Epsom salts

August 25 was the day of the Opiconsivia, a festival held in honor of Ops, the goddess of plenty. Associated with abundance at the time of the harvest, Ops is a goddess of transitions as the seasons change. Choose an August night to take a bath and bring about changes in your own life.

Blend the herbs into the Epsom salts, and fill your bathtub with comfortably warm water. Add the herb-salt mixture, and climb into the tub. Close your eyes and relax, and think about the changes you need to make. What do you need to do differently to bring about transformation? Say *Life transitions and rearranges, starting today, everything changes.* Repeat this as many times as you like while you sit in the water. When you're ready to get out, drain the tub, dry off, and get started with the next phase of your life.

Spell to Influence Others

You'll need:
- A gold candle
- An elder twig

Remember that best-selling book about winning friends and influencing people? It's been a hit for ages because people want to influence others. In addition to being a decent human being, you can work a bit of magic to help expand your range of influence so others will respond to you in the way you deserve.

Light the candle, and say *Influence grow, increasing power, persuasive magic every hour.* Drip some of the melting wax on the tip of the twig, coating it completely, saying *Others will finally listen to me, I'm in control of all I see.* Extinguish the candle, and carry the twig in your pocket, or place it in your office or workstation, to help you influence those with whom you come into contact.

August 27

Broom Spell to Keep Nosy Neighbors Away

You'll need:
- A fork
- A broom
- Salt

Many of us like our neighbors and form solid friendships with them, but if you have a nearby busybody who can't stay out of your business, it's time to do a bit of magic to keep this person away.

Stand inside your front door, or wherever your nosy neighbor typically makes his or her appearance. Tuck the fork securely into the bristles of the broom, and stand it behind the door, with the bristles pointing upward. Sprinkle the salt into the bristles, saying *Nosy neighbor, go away, don't come visit or try to stay. Mind your beeswax, bug me no more, and don't come knocking on my door.*

If your neighbor decides to stop by, touch your hand to the fork before you open the door, and he or she should leave quickly.

Candle Wax Love Magic

You'll need:
- A red candle
- A small bowl of cinnamon

Want to add a bit of zest to your bedroom activities? If you and your partner find yourselves too busy to get any intimacy into your schedule, try this spell to spice things up. Do this working in the evening, in your bedroom, before you turn in for the night.

Sit on your bed and light the candle, thinking about the love you have for your partner and how you're ready to reconnect. Drip some of the melted candle wax into the cinnamon. Give the wax a moment to cool, and before it hardens shape it into a heart, mixing the cinnamon into it. Say *Touching each other, skin on skin, so much love in this room. Let us go back to where we began, that our love may begin anew.*

Once you've shaped your heart and it has firmed up, tuck it under the mattress, and extinguish the candle.

August 29

Buckeye
Good Luck Charm

You'll need:
- A buckeye nut
- A drill
- Red string

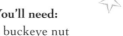

The buckeye, or horse chestnut, is found growing wild in many places, and it typically begins to drop from the trees in late August. The buckeye is associated with good fortune and gambler's luck, and you can gather them and use them in magical charms.

Place the buckeye in your oven on a low temperature, around 200°F, for several hours to dry it out completely. Once it's dry, use your drill to make a hole going all the way through, and thread it on the red string. Tie a knot, and wear it around your neck or hang it in your home when you need a little extra good luck to come your way.

August 30

Spell for
Giving Thanks

You'll need:
- A feast prepared for friends and family
- A bonfire
- Paper and pens

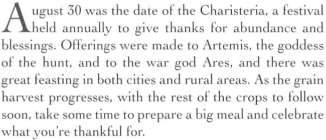

August 30 was the date of the Charisteria, a festival held annually to give thanks for abundance and blessings. Offerings were made to Artemis, the goddess of the hunt, and to the war god Ares, and there was great feasting in both cities and rural areas. As the grain harvest progresses, with the rest of the crops to follow soon, take some time to prepare a big meal and celebrate what you're thankful for.

Invite your favorite people to join you for a big dinner. Try to prepare seasonal food, like home-baked bread or roasted vegetables from your garden. Ask everyone to leave a single bite on his or her plate. Light the bonfire, and invite each person to write something for which he or she thankful on a piece of paper. One at a time, have each guest toss the last bite of food into the fire, saying *I am thankful for the food I have eaten, I am thankful for this fellowship, and I am thankful for* [WHATEVER THEY HAVE WRITTEN].

Once everyone has contributed their offering and shared, add the papers into the fire, and watch as the ashes are carried away in the smoke.

August 31

Thyme Spell to Prevent Nightmares

You'll need:
- Dried thyme leaves
- An amethyst crystal
- A silver cloth

A number of herbs are associated with sleeping and dream states. If you find yourself suffering from regular nightmares, make this simple herb sachet to help keep the bad dreams at bay. Try to do this working on a Monday night, right before you go to bed, but if you've been having disruptions in your sleep cycle, do it at any time.

Place the thyme and the amethyst in the center of the cloth, and tie the corners shut to create a small bag. Tuck the bag under your pillow, and say *Restful sleep and restful dreams, peaceful thoughts in my mind. Restful dreams and restful sleep, peace and quiet I shall find.*

Lie down and inhale the fragrance of the thyme as you drift off to sleep.

September

SEPTEMBER IS KNOWN AS THE HARVEST season in many areas. Crops and fields are overflowing, orchards are full with abundance, nuts are dropping from the trees, and even our home gardens are providing us with delicious foods. However, along with the harvest comes the knowledge that the earth is slowly dying, and that soon the chilly nights will return.

The evenings are cool and crisp with the smell of burning leaves upon the air, and it's the season of the autumn equinox. This period of equal hours of darkness and light is a time of balance. September's spellwork focuses on that harmony, along with the symbolism of the fall harvest.

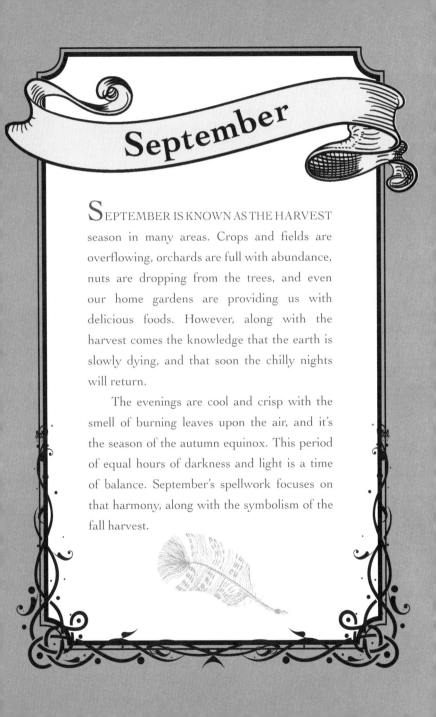

September 1

Acorn
Love Divination

You'll need:
- A red marker
- Two acorns
- A bowl of warm water

Acorns are plentiful in late summer and early fall, and they're often associated with power and strength. Fortunately, they also come in handy for divination, especially in matters of the heart. If you're currently in a relationship and wish to see where it's going, use a pair of acorns and this simple spell to find out. If possible, use acorns plucked directly from an oak tree, rather than collected from the ground. If you can, do this spell on a Thursday, which is associated with the god Thor, because oak trees feature prominently in his legends.

Write your initials on one of the acorns and your lover's on the other. Place them side by side in the center of the water, and close your eyes. Say *Two lovers, you and me, show me where our love will be. Two lovers, me and you, I need to see what our love will do.*

Open your eyes and see where the acorns are. Are they still floating together? If so, it means the relationship is solid. If they're on opposite sides of the bowl, it could indicate that you'll eventually part ways. However, if one is still in the water and the other is floating away, it's a sign that you'll have some obstacles to overcome if you want the love match to survive.

September 2

Spell to Change Someone's Opinion of You

You'll need:
- A banana
- Cloves
- A bowl
- Honey

Ever wish you could change someone's mind about you? Maybe you got off to a rocky start; perhaps you just made a poor first impression. For whatever reason, he or she doesn't think too highly of you. In addition to showing by words and actions that you're not all bad, you can do this spell for a little magical nudge toward resolving the issue.

Peel the banana and stud it with the cloves, saying *[NAME], your regard is valuable to me. I will you not to think ill of me.*

Place the banana in a bowl, and drizzle honey over it. Say *[NAME], if you get to know me, you'll see that I am worthy of your esteem. I will you not to think ill of me.*

Dig a hole in your yard and bury the banana. Next time you see this person, be kind, and you'll notice a difference in the way he or she responds.

September 3

Sandalwood
Business Charm

You'll need:
- A knife
- A citronella candle
- Sandalwood oil

The first Monday in September is Labor Day, which is a celebration of the contributions the workforce has made to America. If you're hoping to increase business at your own workplace, do this spell over Labor Day weekend. This working uses citronella, which not only helps keep mosquitos away, but is also known for drawing business traffic.

Use the knife to inscribe dollar signs on the candle. Drizzle a bit of the sandalwood oil on top of the candle, and light it. Say *Hard work pays off, dedication pays off, effort pays off, organization pays off. Customers come through these doors, business come through these doors, money come through these doors, profit come through these doors.*

Let the candle burn out on its own.

September 4

Spell to
Make New Friends

You'll need:
• Colorful embroidery floss

In many areas, the beginning of September means children are heading back to school, and this can be a challenge. If your youngster is the new kid at school, or simply someone who struggles to make friends in an unfamiliar situation, use a bit of magic in tandem with the mundane to help things develop.

Braid the embroidery floss together to make bracelets, and as you do so, say *New friends and old friends, found every day. Old friends and new friends, coming to stay. As acquaintances grow and two become one, we join together in friendship and fun!*

Let your child wear the bracelets to school so he or she can share them with classmates and other potential friends.

September 5

Spell for
Luck in Legal Issues

You'll need:
- A purple candle
- Nine marigold flowers
- A cloth drawstring bag

If you're facing some sort of legal matter, whether criminal or civil, it never hurts to use a bit of magic to tip the scales of justice in your favor. Do this spell the night before a legal decision.

Light the candle, and place the marigolds in a circle around it. Say *Justice and fairness come to me, in this matter of the courts. Fair and favorable decisions come to me, in this matter of the courts.*

Crush the marigold flowers in your hand, place them in the bag, and pull the drawstring tight. Sleep with the bag under your pillow and carry it in your pocket the next day until the decision is made.

September 6

Corn Magic
Prosperity Spell

You'll need:
- A green candle
- An unshucked ear of corn

In some Native American tribes, September is the season in which the ripened corn is celebrated. Gratitude is offered for the abundance of the fields and orchard, and it is a time of welcoming prosperity. You can do a bit of corn magic yourself to bring seasonal prosperity into your own life.

Light the candle, and say *The corn is ripe, the fields are full, and the land is prosperous.*

Shuck the corn, saying *My life is full, my life is abundant, and I welcome prosperity whenever it comes to me.*

Let the candle burn out on its own. Bury the corncob in your yard, but hang the silks and husks in your kitchen to draw in prosperity.

September 7

Apple Pie
Love Spell

You'll need:
- Your favorite apple pie recipe and ingredients
- Nutmeg
- Vanilla ice cream

Apples are abundant this time of year, and are associated with a number of magical purposes, including love. Why not do a bit of kitchen witchcraft, and bake a pie to help ease the way into a potential lover's heart?

Prepare the pie according to the recipe, but don't add the top layer of crust yet. Sprinkle the nutmeg on top of the apples, in a heart shape, saying *Apples so sweet, apples in a pie, apples for my lover, the apple of my eye.*

Add the top crust and bake your pie. When it's cooled off, offer a slice to your potential lover, topped with a scoop of vanilla ice cream.

September 8

Garlic Spell to Protect Your House From Storms

You'll need:
• A large head of garlic

Everyone knows garlic helps to protect us from vampires, but odds are good that you don't encounter too many of them on a regular basis. Fortunately, garlic also comes in handy for other purposes. In particular, you can use it to protect your home from storms. If you've been growing garlic in your garden, you should have a good crop of it by now. If you didn't grow your own, pick some up at your local farmer's market.

Slice the top off the head of garlic, exposing the tops of the cloves. Peel the cloves, and walk around your house in a clockwise direction. As you do, rub the sliced end of a clove on each doorframe and windowsill. While you do this, say *Wind cannot hurt us, wind cannot harm us. Rain cannot hurt us, rain cannot harm us. Lighting cannot hurt us, lightning cannot harm us.*

Once you've finished, take the remains of the cloves and bury them in your garden or in a pot of fresh soil in a sunny spot, so you can grow new garlic for next year.

September 9

Antler Spell
for Masculine Energy

You'll need:
- A gold candle
- An antler

Each September, there's a celebration in the rural English village of Abbots Bromley called the Horn Dance. This event has become famous, as it's a bit of a throwback to early Renaissance-era festivals, and dancers carry large sets of reindeer antlers. You probably don't have access to a reindeer, but if you can find another sort of antler, do this spell to boost the energy levels of the man in your life. Do this working at sunrise.

Stand facing east so you can watch the sun as it rises, and light the candle. Say *Power of the sun, masculine strength; give [NAME] the power he needs.*

Hold the antler in both hands and raise it up to the sun, saying *Vitality and virility, sunlight rays; give [NAME] the power he needs.*

Let the candle burn out on its own, and bury the antler on the individual's property. If he lives in your home, tuck it under his bed.

September 10

Harvest Moon Spell to Reap What You Have Sown

You'll need:
- A silver candle
- Wheat stalks

The full moon in September is known as the Harvest Moon, and it is a time for reaping what we have sown. We are gathering and collecting the fruits of our labors, measuring that which we planted months ago. Whether your reaping is physical, mental, or spiritual, now is a good time to harvest what you have tended all season long. Do this working after dark, once the moon has risen.

Light the candle, and say *It is a time of gathering, a time of harvesting, a time of blessings. Today, I gather the rewards of my labor, pluck the fruits of my harvest, and embrace the results of my effort.*

Pull a few seeds from the heads of the wheat stalks. Hold them in your hand, and think about all the things in your life that you can harvest this season. Sprinkle them on the ground around you, saying *Under the harvest moon, I count my many blessings, in the season of the harvest.* Do this nine times, until all the seeds are on the ground.

Hold the empty stalks up to the moon, and say *As the winter months come to pass, I will continue to show gratitude for what I have. Come spring, I will sow more seeds, and feel grateful once again in the fall.*

Let the candle burn out on its own.

September 11

Spell to Memorialize Victims of Mass Tragedy

You'll need:
- White tealight candles
- Rosemary

Unfortunately, in today's world sometimes people are victims of large-scale tragedy, whether manmade or a natural disaster. This affects survivors in different ways. For many of us, there is value in remembrance, even if we didn't know the people who were lost. Do this spell at noon, when the sun is at its peak.

Light the tealights. If you would like to assign one to each victim individually, do so, or you can simply assign them to groups—one for men, one for women, one for children, and so on. As you light each one, say *You are gone but not forgotten, you will be remembered in death as you were in life.*

Hold the rosemary in your hands, and take a deep breath. Say *Rosemary is for remembrance, gone but not forgotten. In memory of this tragedy, your names are remembered with honor.*

Close your eyes and take a few minutes to remember those who were lost, and know that as long as they live in people's hearts and minds, they will never be forgotten.

September 12

Shampoo Spell to Move On From a Lover

You'll need:
- A blue candle
- Spearmint oil
- Your favorite shampoo

A broken heart can be devastating, emotionally and physically. While it's tempting to just bury our sorrows in a gallon of ice cream, or to crawl under the blankets for a month or two, it's also pretty empowering when we finally decide it's time to move on. To put an ex-lover behind you once and for all, do this spell first thing in the morning, when you get ready to take your shower.

Light the candle, and say *It is time to heal, it is time to mend, it is time to move on.*

Add a few drops of the spearmint oil into your shampoo, and swirl it in a clockwise direction to blend it. Get in the shower, with the water as warm as you like, and wash your hair. As you scrub your hair and scalp with the shampoo, say *I have healed, I have mended, I have moved on. You no longer haunt my heart and soul, as I have washed you away.*

Rinse the shampoo, watch it go down the drain, and move on with your life.

September 13

Spell for Personal Success

You'll need:
- An orchid
- A purple cloth bag
- Bay leaves

Got a personal goal you're ready to achieve? Maybe you want to finally get your degree, lose ten pounds, or run your first marathon. Whatever it is, use this working to help boost your odds of success. Do this spell on a Sunday, if possible.

Hold the orchid in your hand, and say *I will attempt, I will accomplish, I will succeed. Triumphant endings are what I need.*

Place the orchid in the bag, and add the bay leaves, saying *In my abilities I believe, nothing will stop me, I will achieve.*

Carry the bag in your pocket while you work on your new endeavors.

September 15

Hopscotch Spell to Make Decisions

You'll need:
- Chalk
- A sidewalk
- A stone

Did you ever play hopscotch when you were a kid? It's a lot of fun, and it can be even more fun if you do it as an adult. Use this working if you're facing difficult decisions and can't make up your mind.

Use the chalk to draw a hopscotch board with ten spots on the sidewalk. In the different spots, write down one of your options—if you have two choices, write each one five times. If you have three, write two of them three times, and the last one in four spaces, and so on. Once you've filled each space with an option, stand at the beginning of your hopscotch board.

Close your eyes and hold the stone in your hand. Say *Decisions to make, choices to choose. Help me pick, so I won't lose.*

Gently toss the stone and open your eyes to see where it landed. Skip over to it to pick it up, and know that the option in that space is the right choice.

September 14

Spell to Help You Remember Information

You'll need:
- A piece of fluorite, clear quartz, or citrine

We're bombarded with information almost constantly, so when we need to remember something really important, it's sometimes hard to separate it from all the trivia in our brains. Many people believe that certain crystals can help store information, so if you have something specific you want to remember, do this simple spell to give your brain a boost.

Hold your crystal in your cupped hands, and whisper the information you wish to remember into the stone nine times. After the last time, hold the crystal to your forehead, close your eyes, and say *Information, memory mine, come back as needed and I'll be fine.*

Keep the crystal with you, and when you need to recall the information, close your eyes and hold it to your forehead to jog your memory.

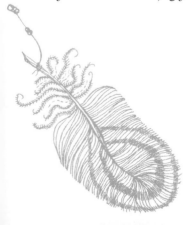

September 16

Spell to Reconnect With an Old Flame

You'll need:
- A red candle
- Your favorite lipstick*
- A photo of your ex

Perhaps you bumped into your ex-lover at the grocery store, and he or she looks really good. Maybe your high school sweetheart is divorced and just friended you on social media. There are times when it's pretty tempting to rekindle an old flame, and a bit of magic can certainly help move things along. Try to do this working on a Friday, right before you go to bed.

Light the candle, and say *I miss you and need you, I want you in my life. Time has passed, and wounds have healed, we've moved beyond the strife.*

Apply the lipstick, and kiss the photo of your ex. Say *Come back to my life, come be mine, and we'll make it work this time.*

Let the candle burn out on its own, and tuck the photo under your pillow.

If you don't own lipstick, lip balm is a perfectly acceptable substitute.

September 17

Spell to Overcome Being Intimidated

You'll need:
- A black candle
- A black-and-white photo of the person
- A red marker

We've all encountered people that are a little intimidating. We worry that they're smarter, richer, or more beautiful than we are, or they just have a commanding presence that makes us feel inadequate. Sometimes the problem is not with them, but rather our own self-perception. If someone makes you feel intimidated—whether on purpose or unintentionally— do this working to help you overcome it. Try to do this spell in the week following the full moon, if possible.

Light the candle, and say *Feelings of intimidation, I banish you. Feelings of inadequacy, I banish you. Feelings of shortcomings, I banish you.*

Place the photo in front of you, and use the marker to decorate it. Draw silly eyebrows, flowers in the person's hair, a big goofy smile, and so on. Have fun with it. Make it as ridiculous as you like. When you're done, look at your artwork with pride, and say *You no longer have power over me, and I will smile when I see you.*

Extinguish the candle, and put the photo away where no one will ever see it. Next time you encounter the person, smile at them as you remember your drawing, and you won't be intimidated any more.

September 18

Spell for
Long-Distance Love

You'll need:
- A map that includes your location and your lover's
- A red marker
- Red heart stickers

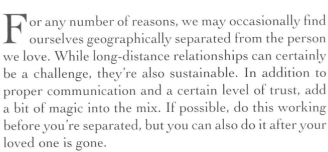

For any number of reasons, we may occasionally find ourselves geographically separated from the person we love. While long-distance relationships can certainly be a challenge, they're also sustainable. In addition to proper communication and a certain level of trust, add a bit of magic into the mix. If possible, do this working before you're separated, but you can also do it after your loved one is gone.

Place the map in front of you, and circle your location and your lover's. Draw a line connecting the two circles, saying *Physically we may be far apart, but you are always in my heart.*

Decorate the red line with the stickers, forming a chain of hearts between you. Say *Distance doesn't matter for me and you, love will always connect us two.*

Fold up the map and keep it under your mattress.

September 19

New Home
Happiness Spell

You'll need:
- A brand-new bowl full of fresh fruit
- Fresh rosemary, basil, and oregano branches
- A vase full of water

When you move into a new home, it's natural to want to be happy there. After all, it's where your family is going to live for a good long time. Do this working immediately after you've moved some of your furniture into the place, but before you sleep there for the first time.

Stand in your new kitchen, and place the bowl of fruit on the counter. Invite the entire family to gather around. Say *Happy new home, happy new hearth. We are blessed with this new place to live, and we will be happy here.*

Place the herbs in the vase one at a time, saying *Rosemary is for the memories we will create, basil is for our prosperity soon to come, and oregano for the joyful strength of our family ties.*

Keep the fruit bowl on your new counter for healthy snacks, and use the herbs in your family's first meal in the new house.

September 20

Autumn Equinox
Spell for Balance

You'll need:

- A white stone
- A black stone
- A collection of fresh autumn leaves

Around September 20, the autumn equinox, or Mabon, falls. Like its spring counterpart, this is a time of equal hours of light and dark, a season of balance. But as the days begin to grow shorter, you may be feeling a little wobbly, both physically and spiritually. Do this working to help you get a bit of seasonal balance, so you can get back on track as the nights grow colder and longer.

Go outside and sit on the ground. Hold the stones together, saying *Black and white, dark and light, balance finding me. The summer is done, and winter comes, balance finding me.*

Place the stones on the ground in front of you, and consider all the balance you have — or still need to find — in your life. Close your eyes for a moment, holding the leaves in your hands. Smell them, and take in the aroma of fall as it surrounds you. Say *As the days grow short, and the cold arrives, I'll find balance and joy within my life.*

Toss up the leaves in the air, and let them fall down on you before you get up to go home.

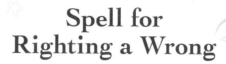

September 21

Spell for
Righting a Wrong

You'll need:
- A white candle
- A piece of paper and a pen
- Three white feathers

September 21 is the International Day of Peace, and it's a good time to bring a bit of peaceful resolution into our own lives. If you've wronged someone and you're ready to extend the olive branch but aren't sure how, do this working to pave the way for reconciliation.

Light the candle, and say *I have made errors and I was wrong. The mistakes I made are mine to own.*

On the paper, write down the name of the person you've wronged, and what you did. Place the paper under the candle, saying *[NAME], I am sorry, by this candle's light, I ask permission to make things right.*

Finally, tuck the three feathers under the candle, on top of the paper. Say *I ask you to give me a second chance, please; I'll do what I must to bring us peace.*

Extinguish the candle, and the next time you see the person, make it clear that you're ready to fix your mistakes.

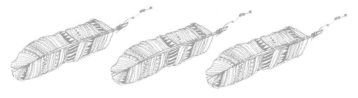

September 22

Spell to Get an Ex-Lover Out of Your Life

You'll need:

- Three photos of your ex
- Black paint and a paintbrush

Ideally, when a relationship ends, we would all just go on about our business and act like adults. Unfortunately, some people can get a little clingy, and won't take no for an answer. If your relationship is over but the other person won't stop calling, texting, or driving by your house, do this working to push him or her out of your life.

Place the photos in front of you, and speak to them firmly. Say *You are not welcome, you are not wanted. Our time together has ended, and you need to move on without me.*

Paint a big X over the first photo, saying *[NAME], you are gone from my life. Paint an X over the second photo, and say [NAME], you are gone from my heart.* Finally, put an X on the last photo, and tell it *[NAME], you are gone from my mind.*

Take the photos somewhere far from your home, and bury them.

September 23

Libra Spell for Harmony at Work

You'll need:
- A business card or letterhead
  from your workplace
- Rose oil
- Frankincense oil

The Zodiac sign of Libra kicks off on September 23, and it's an air sign that represents balance, peacemaking, and diplomacy. If you're watching things start to go badly at work—and you are simply a spectator who is not directly involved—use this spell to try bringing about a peaceful solution to the conflict.

Dab a bit of the rose oil on the business card, and say *For the greater good, let peace and harmony prevail.*

Dab some frankincense oil, saying *For the greater good, let diplomacy and fairness prevail.*

Fold the card three times. Say *We are all working for a common cause, and mutual respect must prevail.* Hide the card somewhere at work so people will begin to get along again.

September 24

Walnut Wishing Spell

You'll need:
- A black marker
- A walnut
- A nutcracker

Walnuts are abundant in the fall, and in most traditions of folk magic they are associated with granting wishes. If you have a walnut tree nearby, gather a few nuts and make some wishes of your own.

Write your wish on the walnut shell. Hold the nut tightly in your hand, close your eyes, and say *Walnuts and magic, and dreams come true. Wishes can happen; I know they do.*

Crack the walnut, and eat the meat inside. Bury the pieces of the shell in the ground. Repeat this working for up to seven days to make your wish come true.

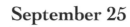

September 25

Ginger Oil
Money Spell

You'll need:
- A piece of ginger root
- 8 ounces base oil

Ginger is a root found in a number of cooking applications, but it also has some practical magical uses because it's associated with money and abundance. Use ginger root blended with oil to bring money your way. For your base, use an unscented oil like jojoba, grape-seed, or safflower.

Grate the ginger finely, and add it to the base oil. As you blend it, say *Money and abundance come my way, fill my purse with coin. Money and abundance for every day, fill my purse with coin.*

Dip your finger in the oil and trace dollar signs on the outside of your wallet, purse, or piggy bank.

September 26

Sapphire Spell for Comfort During Illness

You'll need:
- A silver candle
- Thyme, fresh or dried
- A sapphire

The birthstone for September is the bright blue sapphire, which is customarily associated with divination, prophecy, and healing. If there's someone in your life who's been ill, you can do this working to help provide some relief and comfort during the sickness.

Light the candle, and sprinkle the thyme around it. Hold the sapphire between your palms. Say *Healing magic, sapphire's power, bring relief of pain. Healing magic, sapphire's power, bring comfort again.*

Let the candle burn out on its own, and place the sapphire in the sick person's hospital room or bedroom.

September 27

Rotten Apple Banishing Spell

You'll need:
- A sharp knife
- A red apple
- Black tissue paper

If there's something—or someone—in your life you want to get rid of, a good old-fashioned banishing spell can be remarkably useful. Apples are in season during the fall, and while they are extremely handy for divination and attraction magic, apples also eventually rot and decay. Use an apple to eliminate problem people or issues from your life.

Use the knife to inscribe into the skin of the apple the name of the person—or the type of issue—you need to get rid of. After you've done so, cut the apple in half, making sure you slice through the name. Wrap the two halves in the tissue paper, dig a hole, and bury them somewhere far from your home. As the apple decays in the earth, your problems will gradually go away.

September 28

Spell for Emotional Strength

You'll need:
- A gold candle
- Equal parts St. John's wort, fennel seed, and nutmeg

Ever feel like you just couldn't get through one more day of challenges? Like you were shouldering the weight of the world? As though everyone depended on you to be the strong one? It gets exhausting, but sometimes the strong people are that way because others need to lean on them. If you're getting run-down mentally because other people are depending on you, do this spell to give yourself a little extra emotional strength. Try to time it for a Sunday night, before you go to bed.

Light the candle, and say *I am the one on whom others depend, but my emotional stamina is starting to end. Give me strength, that I may soar, give me the strength to get through one day more.*

Blend the herbs together on a plate, and drip a bit of the melted candle wax into them. As it cools but before it hardens, shape it into a small disk. Place the disk under your pillow as you go to sleep. Hold it in your hands each morning before you get up to start your day so you can absorb the strength of the herbs.

September 29

Crayon Spell for Creative Thinking

You'll need:
- Crayons
- A new coloring book

Everyone loves to color. It's relaxing, and it allows us to express our creativity in a way that's fairly organized but still fun. With the rising popularity of adult coloring books, there's something out there for just about everyone. If you have crayons around your house, do this spell to boost your creative spark.

Close your eyes and open the coloring book to a page at random. Open your eyes, and see what you're going to be working. As you get started, use unconventional colors and think outside the box. Make the grass purple, or the sky yellow. Color a pink cow or a bright blue cat. Be adventurous and go outside the lines if you dare! As you're coloring, let your mind clear of everything but the colors, and fill every inch of white paper on the page, all the way to the corners and edges.

Hang your artwork somewhere where you can admire it, and then go create something brand-new, original, and beautiful.

September 30

Spell to Make a Friendship Last

You'll need:
- Equal parts cloves, dried apple, and passionflower
- A bowl
- A clean sock from each friend

If you and your friends are all busy, or some are moving away, it can be hard to maintain a relationship. Do this working to help make a friendship last through thick and thin, no matter what sort of obstacles might get in the way.

Mix up the herbs in the bowl, stirring clockwise, and saying *Friends for life, friends forever, friends of the heart, friends forever.*

Use a spoon to put equal amounts of the herb blend in each sock, and then tie the tops of the socks tightly. Give the socks back to your friends, but make sure no one gets their own sock; everyone should have someone else's. Keep the sock you get someplace safe, and the friendship will be maintained.

October

OCTOBER IS WHEN WE REALLY BEGIN to notice how cool and dark the nights are getting. As the days grow shorter, many people believe the boundary between the mortal world and the spirit realm becomes thinner. In some magical traditions, it's the season of Samhain, the witches' new year. This is also the season when the fields and land go dormant and empty, an end to the annual agricultural cycle. We clean up our gardens so they can winter over, knowing that in spring the endless loop of life, death, and rebirth will begin anew.

This time of year, you may notice things going bump in the night, or feel like you're not completely alone when you're sure you're the only person in the room. Spellwork for October emphasizes working with the spirit world, divination, and communicating with our long departed ancestors. It's a month of transition and change, both in the worldly plane and the metaphysical one.

October 1

Apple Divination
to See Your
Future Lover

You'll need:
- An apple
- A knife
- A mirror

In many rural societies, divination wasn't done with fancy tools. Instead, people used what they had on hand. This time of year, apples are plentiful, so apple divination became a popular pastime. It's believed you can use an apple to see your future lover. Do this spell in a dimly lit room when the lights are out.

Wait until midnight, then cut the apple into nine pieces. Turn off the lights, and begin eating the pieces while you look in the mirror. When you get to the final piece, stop and close your eyes. Say *Reveal to me my lover, his [or her] face reveal to me, reveal to me my lover, his [or her] face I wish to see.*

Throw the last piece of apple over your shoulder, and open your eyes. You should catch a glimpse of your future lover's face in the mirror.

October 2

Spell to Forget
an Old Lover

You'll need:
- Salt
- Dried angelica leaves or root
- A small bottle of water

When we can't forget the loves of our past, it's often difficult to move on and allow ourselves new love in the present. If the recollection of an old lover is creating baggage for you, and it is affecting your current relationships, do this spell to help put those memories behind you.

Add the salt and angelica to the bottle of water. Swirl it vigorously in a clockwise direction to mix up the contents, saying *No more baggage, no more pain, no more trips down memory lane. I release myself so your memory is gone. I give myself permission, it's time to move on.*

Repeat this each night for the next seven nights, continuing to swirl the bottle clockwise. On the morning of the eighth day, pour the water down the drain and throw away the empty bottle.

October 3

Grape Leaf Magic for Prosperity

You'll need:
- A grape leaf
- A silver coin
- Green string

Grapevines are in abundance in October, and this is the season to honor Bacchus and Dionysus, the gods of wine and vineyards. Grapes and their vines are associated with opulence and prosperity, so take advantage of this, and do a bit of money magic.

Wrap the grape leaf around the coin, and tie it with the string to secure it, saying *Fruit and orchards, grapes and vines, prosperity come to me and mine.*

Carry it in your pocket or wallet to bring some extra cash your way.

October 4

Storm Spell
to Ease Your Grief

You'll need:

- An empty bowl
- A black glass bottle

In parts of Scotland, this time of year is associated with a legendary figure known as the Cailleach. She brings storms and destruction, but in her wake, life and hope always return. If you've been grieving for someone* or something that is no longer in your life, use the energy of an October storm to help you move on.

Place the bowl outside on a stormy night to gather rainwater. In the morning, pour the water into the bottle and take it to a place that reminds you of the person for whom you mourn. Hold the bottle close to your heart, and say *[NAME], you are absent but always remembered, you are mourned but always loved, you are gone but always honored.*

Pour the water in a circle around you, working in a clockwise direction, saying *I will remember you, I will love you, I will honor you. To do these things, I will allow myself to move forward and live again.*

When you have finished, take a moment to say good-bye, and return home.

** If you're grieving for someone who has passed away,
you can place the bowl on the person's grave to gather your rainwater,
and collect it the next day.*

October 5

Reconciliation Spell

You'll need:
- A small piece of paper and a pen
- An orange candle

As the old magical year draws to a close, now is a good time to mend any quarrels in which you've been involved. If you've been battling with someone and you need to work toward a harmonious reconciliation, do this spell on a Friday morning to bring about peace.

Write your name on the piece of paper, then write the other person's name so it overlaps and crosses your own. Wrap the paper around the candle, saying *Mend our quarrels, repair what's broken, harmful words once were spoken. Mistakes were made and harm was done, reconciliation has begun.*

Light the candle, with the paper still wrapped around it, and allow it to burn down completely. Once it burns out, bury what's left near your home, and take any additional mundane steps in order to help bring about healing in the relationship.

October 6

Chrysanthemum Magic for Protection

You'll need:
• Potted chrysanthemums

I n October, chrysanthemums are blooming all over the place. Their bright and varied colors have become a staple of the autumn season, and they're often one of the last plants to flower before winter sets in. In some folklore, they're associated with protection, particularly the metaphysical type. If you're worried about ghosts, spirits, or other hauntings swooping into your space this time of year, use chrysanthemums to create an ethereal boundary.

Place a pot of chrysanthemums at each exterior door of your home, beginning at the front steps and working in a clockwise direction. At each door, when you place the pot beside it, say *This home is protected from spirits, and none shall enter without permission.*

Be sure to water your mums periodically so they don't die off!

October 7

Window Washing Spell
for Cleansing

You'll need:
- A gallon of spring water
- Three to five lemons
- Rosemary, fresh or dried

Although spring cleaning is a popular annual ritual for many people, a thorough autumn cleaning of the house is a great idea as well. After all, you're about to be cooped up for a few months over the winter, so why not get your home as spotless as possible before you have to close up everything for the season? Use this simple window-washing spell to get things tidy not just physically, but metaphysically as well.

Heat the water on your stovetop, and quarter the lemons. Squeeze them into the water, and then add the rosemary. Bring the water to a low boil, reduce heat, and simmer for ten minutes. Allow the water to cool, then pour it into a bucket or a spray bottle. Use it to wash your windows inside and out, and as you clean them, say *Summer has ended, fall is passing, winter is on its way. The windows shine to let the light in, and all is clean today!*

When you're finished, pour out the dirty water somewhere away from your home.

October 8

Blood Moon Water Divination

You'll need:
• A silver candle
• A bowl or cauldron full of water

The full moon in October is known as the Blood Moon because it often has a reddish tinge to it, depending on atmospheric conditions. In some folklore, it's referred to as the Hunter's Moon. Regardless of what you call it, this full moon is perfect for a bit of divination work. Do this at midnight, on the night of the full moon.

Sit outside, and light the candle. Close your eyes, and think about your question. Does it relate to your love life? Your career? Perhaps you just want to know what's going on in general. Open your eyes, and drip the melted candle wax into the water. Watch what shapes the wax forms as it hardens. Write down what you see, and evaluate it the next morning. The shapes should give you an idea of what to look for in the coming weeks. For example, a rose or heart might indicate romance is coming, or the shape of a star could symbolize success. Trust your intuition to tell you what's on the way.

Charm to Protect Yourself from Energy Vampires

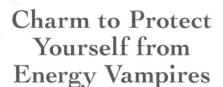

You'll need:
- A yellow candle
- A piece of obsidian

Have you ever encountered an energy vampire? They don't suck your blood, but they drain the energy out of every individual with whom they come into contact. It can be exhausting to be around this type of person, so create a charm to protect yourself.

Light the candle, and hold the obsidian between your hands. Imagine it forming a protective shield around you, your emotions, and your energy, keeping them safe from people who might make you feel drained. Say *My energy is mine, you will not take it. My feelings are mine, you will not have them. My strength is mine, you will not touch it. I am safe from you, and you have no influence on me.*

Carry the obsidian with you, especially if you know you'll be around the energy vampires in your life.

October 10

Pumpkin Spell for Abundance

You'll need:
- A small baking-size pumpkin
- A piece of paper and a pen
- Honey

In October, pumpkins are pretty much everywhere. They're associated with growth and abundance, with their long, trailing tendrils and bright orange blossoms. Pumpkins are perfect for long-term magic, because as the unpicked ones decompose, their seeds make their way into the soil. This means it's not uncommon to find rogue vines growing each year, even if you haven't actually planted pumpkins. If you have a garden, use this simple spell to bring prosperity to your life all year long.

Cut the top off the pumpkin, and scoop out the meat and seeds. Separate them, and set aside the meat for another use. Write on the piece of paper what sort of abundance you'd like to bring into your life, and then place the paper inside the pumpkin. Add the seeds back into the hollow pumpkin, drizzle them with the honey, and put the top back on. Dig a hole in your garden, and bury the entire thing to bring abundance your way.

October 11

Spell for Gratitude

You'll need:
- Rose oil
- A glass of wine or grape juice

The Meditrinalia festival was observed each year on October 11, and it was a time to give thanks for the abundance of the grape harvest. After all, a healthy grape harvest meant lots of wine of a good vintage. Do this spell in the evening, at sundown.

Dab a bit of the rose oil on your wrists and throat, and raise your glass to the skies. Say *I offer thanks to the earth for the things that grow, and thanks to the cool breezes of inspiration. I offer thanks to the rains that wash away troubles, and thanks to the sun for warmth.*

Take three sips of the wine, and pour the rest into the soil, saying *I return to you what came from you, so next year's harvest will be abundant as well.*

Leave the glass outside overnight, and wash it in the morning.

October 12

Fig Spell
for Male Potency

You'll need:
- A red ribbon
- Two ripe figs
- A branch from a fig tree

Depending on where you live, figs tend to ripen on their trees anywhere from August through the middle of autumn. Long associated with male virility, figs are useful for spellwork that will increase a man's potency. In addition to this working, be sure to consult a healthcare professional to rule out possible medical causes of any problems.

Use the ribbon to tie the figs to the base of the branch, saying *Potent and male, masculine power, virile and strong.*

Tuck the branch and the figs under the mattress for seven days to help eliminate problems with impotence.

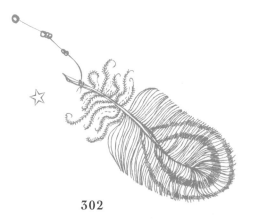

October 13

Spell to Recover from Destruction

You'll need:
- A bonfire
- A pyrite stone

No one likes to think about it, but there are times when destructive forces come into our lives. Whether it's a storm, floods, an earthquake, or some other natural disaster, it can be a challenge to recover. In addition to all the mundane things you have to deal with, like physical rebuilding or repairs, destruction can also take an emotional toll. Fire is one of the best-known destroyers, but unlike other mechanisms, it also creates new beginnings. Use this working to help you heal from the physical destruction of your home or belongings.

Stand in front of the fire, and watch the flames. Think about the things in your life that were destroyed, and know that it's okay to miss them. Hold the pyrite in your hand, extended toward the fire. As you feel the stone begin to warm, say *Destruction came into my life, and took away things I loved. My life changed in that moment of loss. It is now time for me to move forward. I will make new things where the old were lost. I will rebuild new things where the old were torn down. I will live my life with passion and creativity, and tonight, I begin anew.*

Carry the pyrite stone in your pocket, or wear it in a piece of jewelry, as you begin rebuilding your life.

October 14

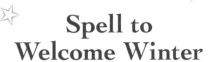

Spell to
Welcome Winter

You'll need:
- Allspice and cinnamon
- An apple, sliced into wedges

Even though it's only October, today is the day of the Norse Vinternatsblot celebration, which marked the onset of winter in the northern European world. It may still be autumn where you live, but as the nights grow cold and long, it's a reminder that the seasons are always changing. Welcome the coming winter by doing this spell after dark, when the night is cool and brisk.

Sit outside in the darkness and look up at the stars. Mix together the allspice and cinnamon, and dip the first wedge of the apple in it. Before you take your first bite, say *Farewell to autumn, and welcome to winter. The seasons change, and so do I. As winter moves in, I bring to my home joy, abundance, and blessings.*

Repeat this for each wedge of the apple until all are gone. Think about the blessings you hope to receive in the coming months.

October 15

Spell to Help With Decision Making

You'll need:
- Index cards and a pen
- A feather

It's a given that the more options we have, the harder it can be to make a decision. When you have multiple choices before you, how do you know you're picking the right one? Sometimes it helps to just trust our instincts, but often it takes a little metaphysical nudge to convince us. If you have a selection of opportunities but aren't sure which one to go with, do this working, preferably on a Wednesday, to help you come to the right conclusion.

Write your options on the index cards, so each one has a potential choice on it. Place them around you on the floor. Hold the feather in your dominant hand, and close your eyes. Slowly turn in a circle—don't go too fast, or you'll get dizzy—three times. When you stop, hold the feather above your head, eyes still closed, and say *Decisions, decisions that must be made. I could use a little aid. From my mind and spirit through my hand, let me see where my choice will land.*

Let go of the feather, then open your eyes. The card nearest to where the feather landed is the right choice.

October 16

Spell to Recover from Emotional Trauma

You'll need:
- A white candle
- A piece of paper and a pen
- A fireproof bowl or cauldron

Human emotions can be very fragile. When we experience emotional trauma, we can respond in different ways, but generally we establish coping mechanisms to help us deal. Some people put their trauma behind them and never think of it again. Others need help moving forward because it impacts their lives for years. If you've suffered some sort of emotional trauma, do this working on a Monday to help you find peace.

Light the candle, and spend a few minutes watching the flame. Think about how your trauma has affected your life, and decide you're ready to put it into the past for good. Write the source of your hurt on the paper, and say *It is time for me to release you. It is time for me to release myself. It is time for healing to begin.*

Fold the paper three times, and touch it to the flame. Drop it into the fireproof bowl, and let the words and your pain burn away. As the paper burns, say farewell to the root cause of your trauma. Once it's gone, extinguish the candle. Dispose of the ashes in a moving body of water, or bury them somewhere far from your home.

October 17

Spell for Home Stability

You'll need:
• One stone to represent
each member of the household
• A brown candle
• A blue marker

Home life can be a challenge, especially if you're raising a family, working, going to school, and so on. Throw in big changes, like the birth of a new baby, a move, or a shift in your relationship status, and things get disrupted in a hurry. Do this spell to bring a bit of stability back into your life.

Light the candle, and say *The world turns onward, and the sun rises and sets. Changes happen, and life becomes unsettled.*

Write the name of each family member on his or her own stone, and place the stones in front of the candle. Say *We are family and we are strong. Our love will see us through. Stability and permanence will come into our lives. We will make it through, and we will persevere through the storm.*

Extinguish the candle, and place the stones in the room where your family spends the most time together.

October 18

Opal Spell
for Healing

You'll need:
- A blue candle
- An opal set in a piece of jewelry

October's birthstone is the opal, which is associated with healing magic. If you're feeling run-down and exhausted, do this spell using an opal on a necklace or set in a ring or pair of earrings.

Light the candle, and say *Healing light, glowing in my soul. Healing light, cleansing my spirit. Healing light, bringing wellness to my body and mind.*

Hold the opal up to the light, and watch as the flame reflects from the stone. Slowly bring it closer to you, feeling the healing energy travel with it. Put on the jewelry, and hold the stone in your hand, saying *I am healing, I am on the path to wellness, I will be whole again once more.*

Extinguish the candle, and wear your opal until you begin feeling rejuvenated again.

October 19

Spell to
Silence a Busybody

You'll need:
- A photo of the busybody
- A piece of tape

We've all met them: people who just aren't completely happy until they're all up in your personal affairs. And the more involved they get, the worse they can make things for you. This is when a bit of magic can be extremely practical, as it gets them out of your business while still maintaining the relationship.

Place the photo in front of you, and stick the tape over the individual's mouth. As you do, say *It's my business, so you stay out. With this tape, I close your mouth. Mind your own business and stay out of mine, keep yourself silent, and we'll get along fine.*

Put the photo someplace safe until your relationship with the busybody improves.

October 20

Throwing the Shoe
Divination Spell

You'll need:
• Your right or left shoe

In parts of the Scottish Highlands, there is a divinatory tradition referred to as throwing the shoe, and it's exactly what it sounds like. Use the shoe from your dominant foot, preferably the pair that you've been wearing all day, and do this spell at sunset.

Stand outside your home. Hold the shoe in your dominant hand, and say *What's in the future? The shoe shall show. Reveal to me what I must know.* Throw the shoe as high in the air as you possibly can—the original tradition involved lobbing it over the house, but do this only if you're sure you won't end up having to climb on the roof to retrieve your footwear.

Take a look at how the shoe has landed to get an idea of what the future holds. If it's pointing so the toes are closest to your house, it means you're not going anywhere anytime soon. Toes pointing away indicate there's a journey in the near future. The sole on the ground means you've got stability and security, but the sole pointing up is an indicator that things are shaky and unstable. If the shoe lands on its side, watch out for some completely unexpected news coming your way.

October 21

End of Harvest Prosperity Spell

You'll need:
- A handful of corn kernels
- A dollar bill
- A green drawstring bag

The harvest season is winding down, and the fields will soon be dry and barren. Although the season of abundance and prosperity is coming to an end, we can still use a bit of extra blessings this time of year. Do this spell using corn kernels; if you don't have those handy, you can use squash seeds, beans, or other goodies from your garden.

Place the corn and the money in the bag, and pull the drawstring tight. Hold the bag in both hands, and say *The harvest has ended, my life is abundant. May the blessings of the harvest continue through the coming months. When the nights are cold, may I have good fortune. When my pantry is bare, my I have food to eat. When my wallet is empty, may money come my way. Abundance is always welcome here.*

Place the bag near your front door to invite prosperity inside.

October 22

Apple Cider Spell to Honor the Dead

You'll need:
- Warm apple cider
- Cinnamon sticks

Many people believe this is the time of the year when the dead are closest to us. Whether it's something going bump in the night, or the feeling that you're not really alone, there is a clear sense that the veil between our world and the spirit realm has thinned a bit. A popular tradition is to honor the dead with offerings, as a way of not only appeasing them, but letting them know they are not forgotten. Do this spell outside, after the sun has gone down.

Pour two mugs of warm cider and add the cinnamon sticks. Close your eyes and think about the people in your life who have passed away, whether recently or in years past. Remember how they made you laugh, and the love you shared. This is the night to honor them. Sip your cider slowly, and as you do, call out the names of those you are remembering. Tell them how you felt about them in life, and how you feel about them now that they have crossed over. After each name, pour a bit of the cider from the second mug onto the ground, and say [NAME], *I remember you this night, and honor your memory.*

Continue until the cider is gone and you have recited all the names. Go back inside, but before you do, turn one last time, look behind you, and say *farewell.*

October 23

Scorpio Spell for Self-Assurance

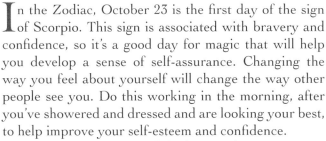

You'll need:
- A purple candle
- A mirror

In the Zodiac, October 23 is the first day of the sign of Scorpio. This sign is associated with bravery and confidence, so it's a good day for magic that will help you develop a sense of self-assurance. Changing the way you feel about yourself will change the way other people see you. Do this working in the morning, after you've showered and dressed and are looking your best, to help improve your self-esteem and confidence.

Light the candle, and look into the mirror. Say *Hey you! You're the kind of person that others listen to. You're the kind of person that others want to like. You're the kind of person others look up to and respect. You're the kind of person that others wish they could be like. Hey you! You are fantastic!*

Admire yourself for a few moments, and realize all the things you just said to yourself are true. Extinguish the candle, and go take on the world.

October 24

Spell to Open Your Third Eye

You'll need:
- Dried mugwort
- Lavender oil

Many people believe we have what's called a third eye, which allows us to have perception beyond ordinary sight, and to see all the potential the world has to offer. In some traditions, the third eye, located in the middle of the forehead, is the center of magical power. Unfortunately, if it's blocked, we can struggle to feel harmony between our mind, body, and spirit. This simple spell will help open your third eye, which will allow you to develop your intuitive abilities and connect to the spiritual world.

Go someplace where you can sit quietly and remain undisturbed. Hold the mugwort in your hands, and take a deep breath, inhaling the aroma. Imagine the scent traveling up to your forehead, and opening up your third eye. Say *I open myself to the wisdom of the universe, I open myself to the knowledge of the ages, I open myself, that I may see.*

Put a small dab of lavender oil on your finger, and anoint the center of your forehead, saying *I can see, I am aware, I am in harmony with myself.*

Sit quietly for a few moments, relaxing, and recognize that you can achieve awareness and clarity.

October 25

Spell to Reconnect with Old Friends

You'll need:
- Individual photos of you and your friends
- A corkboard and pushpins
- Pink yarn

We're all busy with our lives, and sometimes relationships fall by the wayside. Before we know it, it's been months since we've seen or even talked to the people we care about. Worse yet, when it's been a while since we've been in touch, it's even harder to pick up the phone to re-establish contact. Do this working to bring your web of friends back together, especially if you haven't seen each other in some time.

Place the photo of yourself in the center of the corkboard, and arrange the pictures of your friends in a circle around you. Use the pink yarn, in a continuous piece, to connect all of you together, with the pushpins anchoring the yarn in place. As you link yourself to all of your friends, say *Friends forever, through thick and thin, let's connect to each other again. Friends forever, even when we're apart, you're the friends who hold a place in my heart.*

Hang the corkboard where you can see it every day, and each time you walk by it, greet your friends and tell them how much you miss them. Find a way to make the time to reach out soon.

October 26

Spell to Get a
Promotion at Work

You'll need:
- A stairway
- A gold candle and six white tealight candles
- A package of sticky gold stars

There's an opening at work in another department, and you know you'd be perfect for it, but do the hiring managers know? In addition to doing all the mundane tasks, like tidying up your résumé and applying for the position, you can do a bit of magic to help increase your odds of getting those new responsibilities at work. This spell runs over the course of seven days.

Begin by placing the gold candle at the top of the steps, and then putting a tealight on each of the six steps below it. Starting with the bottom candle, each day stick a gold star on the tealight. Light the candle and say *Accomplishments and pride, I am qualified. I've put in my time, this promotion will be mine.* On the second day, move up a step and repeat this, but add two gold stars, and so on. On the seventh day, you'll be at the gold candle on the very top step. Add seven gold stars, saying *My abilities will be seen, I'm the best one for this team. Those who choose me won't regret, when this promotion is what I get.*

At the end of the seventh day, peel off all the gold stars and keep them hidden away in your desk or workspace until you get the promotion.

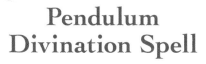

Pendulum Divination Spell

You'll need:
- A piece of paper and a pen
- A pendulum

October is a great time for divination, and if you are facing a dilemma that requires a yes or no answer, a pendulum is the perfect way to figure out what's right. If you don't have a pendulum, you can easily make one by tying a ring or another small weighted item to a string or necklace chain.

Start by drawing a horizontal line on the paper, and at the ends of the line, write the word YES. Next, make a vertical line that crosses through the horizontal, with NO at the top and bottom. Place the paper in front of you, and hold your pendulum loosely over it. Close your eyes, and think of the question or dilemma that you're facing. Say *Yes, no, maybe so, tell me what I need to know,* three times.

Open your eyes and note which way the pendulum is swinging. If it's moving along the horizontal line, the answer is YES. A vertical line swing means NO. A pendulum moving in circles usually indicates that the answer is not defined at this time, or that it's a MAYBE, so try again in a couple of days.

October 28

A Needfire Spell

You'll need:
- A large bonfire
- An offering

In some parts of the ancient Celtic world, people believed that a special fire called the Needfire could bring about magical results. Only to be used in times of great need, the Needfire helped to protect families from plague and pestilence, starvation and exposure, or even marauding tribes. Sometimes it was a place to make offerings—seeds to ensure abundant crop, or a bit of bone from livestock to make sure your herds were safe through the winter. Your needs may not be quite this drastic, but you can still use the Needfire to request the things you require most. Whatever offering you make should be something that holds value to you, not just plucked at random. Home-cooked food or produce you grew yourself is always a good choice. Do this spell after the sun sets.

Stand before the fire, holding your offering, and say *My family needs [*ITEM*] to help us through the season. My family requires [*ITEM*] and no more and no less. I present this offering, consigning it to this fire, in hopes that our needs will be met.*

Drop your offering into the flames, then let the fire go out on its own. Repeat as needed for the next seven nights.

October 29

Cat's Paw
Spell for Gracefulness

You'll need:
- A pink candle
- A tuft of cat fur

Ever watch a cat navigate its way around? Felines seem to have an uncanny sense of balance, even in places that look impossible to traverse, and when they do fall, they land on their feet and saunter away. When you're feeling a bit uncoordinated and awkward, try this spell to help you be more graceful in your daily routine. If you don't have a cat, visit with a friend's furry companion.

Light the candle, and hold the fur in your hand. Say *I am graceful like the cat, I am sleek like the cat, I am elegant like the cat.*

Place the fur on a plate or another hard surface, and drip some of the wax into it. Let it cool just a bit, and then while it's still soft, shape the wax and the fur into an approximation of a paw.

Extinguish the candle, and each night before you go to bed, place the wax paw into the right shoe of whatever footwear you'll be putting on in the morning. When you're ready to get dressed, remove the paw from your shoe and keep it handy for the following evening. The gracefulness of the cat will help you get through the day without stumbling.

October 30

Pumpkin Spell for Protection from Spirits

You'll need:
- A knife
- A pumpkin
- A black candle

It's the time of year when things go bump in the night, and spooky things roam about when we least expect to see them. There's an old tradition of carving lanterns into squash vegetables, which is where the custom of the jack-o'-lantern comes from. If you have a candle and a pumpkin, you can keep the ghosties and poltergeists away.

Cut the top off your pumpkin and scoop out the innards. Carve a face or, if you're not very artistic, words like KEEP OUT on your pumpkin. Place your finished creation on the ground right by your front step, put the candle inside the pumpkin, and light it. Say *Ghosts and haunts aren't welcome here, go back where you belong. The veil is thin but I do not fear, pass this house and just move on.*

Extinguish the candle before you go to bed, and relight it for the next three nights to keep the haunts away.

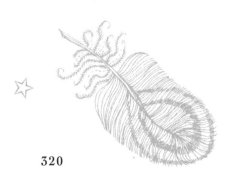

October 31

Witches' New Year's Resolutions

You'll need:
- A white candle
- A piece of paper and a pen
- An envelope

In many magical traditions, October 31 is the celebration of Samhain, which is a holiday marking the end of the old agricultural year. This has given today the nickname of the Witches' New Year, so it's a perfect time to make some resolutions. After all, why wait until the end of December if you can do them now?

Light the candle, and think about what you hope to achieve in the next few months. Write three short-term goals on the paper, and tuck it into the envelope. Seal the envelope and say *As the wheel of the year turns, and the seasons change, I will manifest new hopes and dreams for myself. These are my goals, and I will see them achieved.*

Extinguish the candle, and put the sealed envelope someplace safe. Leave it there until you've accomplished all three things on your list.

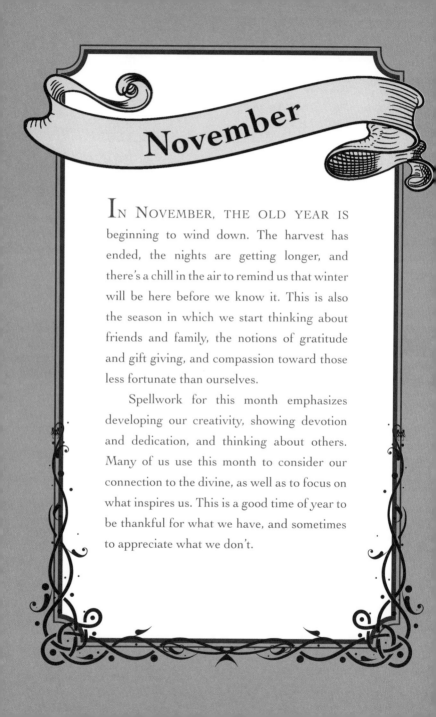

November

IN NOVEMBER, THE OLD YEAR IS beginning to wind down. The harvest has ended, the nights are getting longer, and there's a chill in the air to remind us that winter will be here before we know it. This is also the season in which we start thinking about friends and family, the notions of gratitude and gift giving, and compassion toward those less fortunate than ourselves.

Spellwork for this month emphasizes developing our creativity, showing devotion and dedication, and thinking about others. Many of us use this month to consider our connection to the divine, as well as to focus on what inspires us. This is a good time of year to be thankful for what we have, and sometimes to appreciate what we don't.

November 1

Graveyard
Purification Spell

You'll need:
- Chrysanthemums
- Tealight candles
- Saltwater

The Day of the Dead, el Dia de los Muertos, is observed on November 1 in many Latino communities. It's a time to honor the departed ancestors with flowers, food, and candles, and families make visits to their local cemeteries to clean headstones and speak to the departed. If your loved ones are buried nearby, this is a good day to do a graveyard purification spell. Use saltwater straight from the ocean, if possible, but if you don't live near the coast, you can make your own by blending sea salt with spring water.

Go to the cemetery where your family members are buried. Tidy up the headstones before you begin by trimming back stray weeds and brushing any dirt from the stones. Place the chrysanthemums and candles beside the headstones. As you light the candles, say *Gone but not forgotten, living on in our memories, remembered in our hearts. I purify this space as sacred ground, made holy by our love for you, and our remembrance of your spirit.*

Walk in a circle, moving clockwise, and pour the saltwater on the ground around the grave. If you have multiple relatives buried in adjacent plots, you can make a large circle that includes them all. After you've poured the water, extinguish the candles and tell your family members farewell. Promise to return soon.

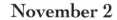

November 2

Soul Cake Spell to Honor the Dead

You'll need:
- Three white candles
- A soul cake

November 2 is the festival of All Souls' Day, in which we honor and pray for the dead. A popular custom is baking soul cakes as gifts for the spirits of the dead. In many parts of Europe, distributing these cakes was the inspiration for modern trick-or-treating. You can find a number of great recipes for soul cakes, so bake the one you like most. Do this spell at night, after sundown.

Light the candles, and place the pastry in front of them. Close your eyes, saying *Souls of the dead, I honor you, but now you must move on. The seasons change, and I honor you, but now you must be gone. Souls of the dead, I pray for you, but now you shall move along.*

Eat the soul cake, and take a moment to think about the souls of those who have passed on this year. When your cake is gone, extinguish the candles.

Fall Bulb Spell for New Beginnings

You'll need:
- A small trowel
- Dried eggshells
- Flower bulbs

If you want to see flowers blooming in your yard next spring, late fall is the time to plant the bulbs. Use this simple spell to plan ahead so you have new things to look forward to after winter ends. Different flowers have different magical associations, so consider carefully what you might like to see. For example, tulips are connected to prosperity and power. Hyacinths represent ongoing love, and irises symbolize our ability to overcome our own self-limiting behavior. What do you want to start anew in the spring?

Dig a small hole with the trowel for each bulb. As you dig, think about what you're planting, and what it means to you both now and in the future. Place the dried eggshells in the bottom of each hole, and then add the bulb. Cover it with dirt, and as you do, say *Bulbs to blossom, bulbs to grow, sprouting in the earth below. Warm through winter, in spring appear, new beginnings always welcome here.*

Once you've planted all the bulbs, be sure to water the soil thoroughly.

November 4

Candle Spell to Balance the Chakras

You'll need:
• Seven candles in the colors of the rainbow

The Hindu celebration of Diwali begins around this time of year, and it is a spectacular festival of lights. Many people believe that the body contains a series of chakras, or energy vortices, that must remain balanced in order to maintain emotional, physical, and spiritual well-being. If you're feeling off-kilter, do this spell to realign your chakras. As you light each candle, say the following:

RED: *I welcome stability and security into my life.*

ORANGE: *I welcome emotional connection into my life.*

YELLOW: *I welcome confidence and power into my life.*

GREEN: *I welcome the ability to give and receive love.*

BLUE: *I welcome the ability to communicate effectively.*

INDIGO: *I welcome intuition and wisdom.*

VIOLET: *I welcome my connection to the divine.*

Take a few moments to close your eyes, and think about the significance of these seven aspects of your life. Let the candles burn out on their own, but if you're still feeling out of balance later, repeat the working as often as necessary.

November 5

Spell to
Eliminate Selfishness

You'll need:
- A pink candle
- Rosemary
- An amethyst crystal

Among the Cherokee people, there is a festival held in early November called Adohuna, which is a time of forming new friendships. It's also a way of celebrating the way the world was before greed and selfishness became so prevalent. If you've been feeling selfish, envious, or greedy lately, and you know you need to make some adjustments, this is a perfect time do some magic.

Light the candle, then rub the rosemary between your palms, inhaling its fragrance. Hold the amethyst loosely in your hands, saying *Envy and greed, go away, I end my internal strife. Selfishness and jealousy have are no longer in my life.*

Allow the candle to burn out on its own, and carry the amethyst with you as a reminder to be a better person when dealing with others.

November 6

Spell to Remove a Rivalry

You'll need:
- A paper towel with your rival's name written on it
- A glass bowl
- Vinegar

I n the United States, the second Tuesday in November is Election Day, and the weeks and months leading up to it are typically full of contention between the various candidates. You may not be running for office, but it's entirely possible you have a rival, either personally or professionally. Here's an easy way to eliminate the competition from your life.

Fold the paper towel into a square, with the name on the outside, and place it in the bowl so the name is facing up. Pour the vinegar over it until it's completely covered. As you do, say *Competition no more, rival no more, opposition no more.*

Let the bowl sit out in the sun for a few days, until the paper begins to break down, then take it someplace far from your home and bury it. The person may still be in your life, but he or she will no longer see you as a rival.

November 7

Mourning Moon Spell to Get Rid of Your Baggage

You'll need:
- Paper and a pen
- An old suitcase
- Basil, black pepper, and marigolds

November's full moon is known as the Mourning Moon or the Fog Moon, and it's a perfect time to do a bit of emotional housecleaning. Now is your chance to get rid of the mental baggage you've been carrying around by getting rid of literal baggage. Hit the thrift store or your grandmother's storage shed to find an old suitcase to use in this working.

Make a list of all the things you want to get rid of. Use as many pieces of paper as you need to, and put them all in the suitcase. Add equal parts of the basil and black pepper, and then add the marigolds. Close the suitcase, get in your car, and drive in any direction for an hour. Find a garbage can, a dumpster, or another disposal site, and put the suitcase in it. As you do, say *I am rid of you for good, I am done with you forever, I am free of you always.*

Drive home without looking in your rearview mirror.

November 8

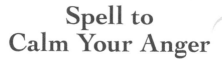

Spell to
Calm Your Anger

You'll need:
- An old ceramic plate
- A black marker
- A black cloth
- A hammer

Ever get so angry that you could just break something? Now is your opportunity to do it. Channel that angry energy into a bit of destruction, and you'll be amazed at how much better you feel afterward.

Hold the plate in your hand, and write on it exactly what you're angry about. Feel free to include things like *My neighbor's dog poops in my yard, my boss is a jerk, and my brother wrecked my car again*. Go crazy with it, and put everything on the plate.

Wrap the plate securely in the black cloth so it's completely covered. Place it on a flat surface, and whack it with the hammer. Go ahead, it'll feel good. In fact, hit it a few times. As you do, say *Anger and rage, go away, I've had enough of you today. I'm moving on, and angry no more, the things that frustrate me go out the door.*

After you've smashed the plate as many times as you need to, take the whole bundle outside, without unwrapping it, and throw it in your trash can to send your anger away.

November 9

Spell to Develop Compassion for Others

You'll need:
- Sandalwood oil
- A red candle
- Dried mistletoe leaf

As the cold weather and the winter holidays draw near, there's often an increased awareness of charitable causes. We're asked to contribute toys for children, warm winter coats, food for the hungry, and all kinds of other things. If you're starting to feel a bit burned out on the requests for assistance, keep in mind that if there wasn't a need, no one would be asking for help. Do this spell to help you develop a little compassion for others during this time of year.

Lightly brush the sandalwood oil over the candle, then roll it in the mistletoe. Light the candle, and focus on the flame. Think about all the charitable causes people have asked you to help out with lately. Are there any that are really close to your heart? Can you show compassion by contributing to just one?

Say *I know there is need, I know there is want. I will show compassion and mercy to those who ask for help, I will show tolerance and patience for those who need my aid. I will learn to be part of the solution, rather than part of a problem. I will give of myself where I can.*

Allow the candle to burn out on its own, and demonstrate your commitment to compassion by offering your time or energy to one of the causes of the season.

November 10

Magic Touch
Success Spell

You'll need:
- A gold candle
- A bottle of nail polish

We all know people who seem to be successful at whatever they attempt. No matter what they do, everything falls into place, and we say they have the magic touch. You can, too, with a simple spell involving your favorite nail polish. If you don't normally paint your nails, go with a clear polish instead.

Light the candle, and hold the bottle of nail polish up to the light. Say *Success is what I need so much, in the power of my touch. All will end as it should it be, I'll make it work, successfully.*

Paint your nails with three coats of polish. When you're done, extinguish the candle, and take on your next big project.

November 11

Spell to
Honor Veterans

You'll need:
• A white candle
• Mementos or photos of military service

In the United States, Veterans Day falls each year on November 11. You probably have a number of veterans in your community, so take a few moments today to honor them with this simple spell. If you are — or a family member is — a veteran, include mementos of the time spent in the service. Do this spell at sundown.

Light the candle, and close your eyes. Think about the people who made sacrifices to join the military, and how we can honor them today. If you are using mementos of your own time in the service, touch each one individually, and say *I honor my brothers and sisters this day, and thank them for their service.* If you are using tokens of a family member's service, touch them and say *Thank you for your service and your sacrifice.*

As the sun sets, think about the future. How will you treat veterans you see once today has passed? Make a commitment to thank them in person, and extinguish the candle.

November 12

Spell to Remove Unwanted Feelings of Attraction

You'll need:
- A black candle
- Equal parts dried lemon verbena, eucalyptus, and marigolds
- A cloth drawstring bag

We've all found ourselves attracted to someone who was completely unsuitable. Perhaps the other person is already attached and in a relationship, or maybe just someone we know is bad for us, but the heart wants what it wants. Do this bath spell to wash away that unwanted attraction to Mr. or Ms. Wrong. Time this, if possible, for the week following the full moon.

Light the black candle, and place it by your bathtub. Put the herbs in the bag, pull the drawstring tight, and hang the bag on the faucet. Fill the tub with water as warm as you can stand, with the water running over the herbs. As the water flows, say *My feelings are unwanted, I will think of you no more. I now shut my heart to you, like I've closed a door.*

Once the tub is full, bathe until the water is cool. Pull the plug and let the water run down the drain, along with your feelings for the individual, and extinguish the candle. Do this for seven nights in a row, and then don't think about him or her again.

November 13

Spell to Make Someone Miss You

You'll need:
- Mementos of the relationship
- A silver bowl
- A sharp knife

Sometimes when that special person isn't around, it makes us feel good to know we are missed. If you're concerned that your loved one might not miss you as much as you miss him or her, do this working outside one night after dark, when you know the individual will be sleeping. Do this spell when the sky is clear and the stars are visible.

Place the mementos in the bowl—they can be photos, gifts, a CD of your favorite songs, and the like. Trace the knife clockwise around the bowl nine times, saying *Think of me, dream of me, remember me, miss me*. The person will dream of you in their sleep, and miss you once he or she wakes.

November 14

Spell for Successful Partnership

You'll need:
- An orange candle
- A photo of yourself
- A photo of the other person

In our professional lives, whether by choice or by necessity, it often comes to pass that we work hand in hand with other people. This can be a challenge, because it's hard to get along with everyone all the time. That's where magic comes in handy. Do this working to bring about a successful business partnership.

Light the candle, and say *Working together, you and me. Working together, harmoniously. Working together, as we should. Working together, for the greater good.*

Drip a bit of melted candle wax on the photos, and use it to attach them together, facing each other. Once the wax has hardened and the photos are secure, extinguish the candle. Keep the attached photos in your desk or workstation to ensure success with your new partner.

November 15

Herbal
Home Blessing

You'll need:
- A white candle
- Dried sage and rosemary
- A bowl

This time of year, the nights are growing dark, and it's not uncommon to feel uneasy. You may not even realize why, but if you start feeling restless, like something is just off, do this simple home purification spell to get things back to normal.

Light the candle, and focus on the idea of purification energy making its way around your home. As you do, rub the sage and rosemary between your palms over the bowl, crumbling them into a fine powder. Walk around your home, focusing especially on doors, windows, and other openings, and drop pinches of the herb blend onto the floor near the baseboards. While you're doing this, say *My house, my place, bless this entire space.*

Use the entire herb blend, and extinguish the candle.

November 16

Spell to Remove Writer's Block

You'll need:
- A flat stone
- A purple marker

Many of us decide in November that it's time to write a novel—after all, there's a month-long event to encourage us. However, about two weeks in, a lot of people stop because they've run out of ideas and inspiration. If you're experiencing writer's block, or the stifling of another kind of creative juices, do this spell to kick-start your inspiration.

Place the stone in front of you, preferably near your work area, whether it's a desk, a studio, or even the kitchen table. Put your hands on top of it, and close your eyes for a moment. Think about all the words you've already written, and know that you will write again. Use the marker to write some of your favorite words on the stone—these can be quotes from your work in progress, or even your book's title.

Say *Creativity come back to me, I need some inspiration. Help me find the words again, with strong communication. I will get past my writer's block, and achieve new clarity. The words will come back to the page, as I will, so it shall be.*

Keep the stone in a place where you can see it, and get back to writing.

November 17

Autumn Dream Truth Spell

You'll need:
- Equal parts cloves, yarrow, and jasmine
- An agate stone
- A cloth drawstring bag

As the nights arrive earlier, it often seems like it's much darker than during the summer months. By this point in the autumn, you may be ready to put on your pajamas and go to bed right after dinner. While this can be inconvenient, if you're hitting the sack early, you might as well take advantage of it and do a bit of dream magic right before you go to sleep. If you feel like you're being lied to, misled, or just not given all the information you're entitled to, do this spell to see what your dreams reveal about the situation.

Add the herbs and the agate stone to the bag, and pull the drawstring tight. Lie with your head on your pillow, eyes closed, and hold the bag so you can smell the herbs. Say *Things are not always what they seem, show me the truth within my dreams. Lies or omissions could be so, show me the truth, I need to know.*

Tuck the bag under your pillow, and as you drift off to sleep, think about the situation. When you wake in the morning, you should have some brand-new insight.

November 18

Spell to Recover from Surgery or Illness

You'll need:
- Three blue candles
- Equal parts cinnamon and cedar shavings
- A charcoal disk for incense, in a fireproof bowl

No one likes to have surgery, but sometimes it can't be helped. In addition to following your doctor's postoperative instructions, you can do a bit of magic to help speed along the healing process. You can also do this working to help provide some relief from chronic conditions.

Light the candles, and blend together the cinnamon and cedar shavings. Light the charcoal disk and add the herbs on top of it so they'll begin to burn. Close your eyes and say *Burn off sickness, burn off pain, healing magic in the flames. Burn off injury, burn off ill, I shall heal, it is my will.*

Allow the candles and incense to burn out on their own. Sprinkle the ashes from the bowl in your yard.

November 19

Topaz
Spell for Loyalty

You'll need:
- A topaz stone
- A pink candle

November's birthstone is topaz, which is associated with a number of magical properties, including honesty, fidelity, and devotion. If you want to inspire allegiance in those around you, do this working to develop loyalty.

Hold the stone in your hands, and close your eyes. Say *Loyalty and honor, fidelity and dedication, honesty and allegiance. I ask that others give to me what I show to them.*

Light the candle, and say *I am loyal, I am true, I ask only the same of others. I am honest, I am dedicated, I wish the same thing in return.*

Extinguish the candle, and carry the topaz in your pocket, or wear it in a piece of jewelry.

November 20

Apple Magic
Good Luck Charm

You'll need:
- An apple
- An apple corer
- A piece of paper and a pen

Apples are often associated with good luck and fortune, so if you want to increase your blessings this time of year, do this spell, and let fate smile upon you.

Wash and core the apple. On the paper, write *Good luck in this apple round, good luck and fortune abound.*

Roll up the paper and tuck it inside the cored apple. Place it someplace in your home where you can see it. If the apple starts to spoil before your luck changes, replace it with a fresh one.

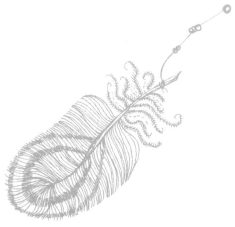

November 21

Hunting Safety Spell

You'll need:
- A marker
- A piece of birch bark
- A yellow ribbon

If you're a hunter, chances are good that this time of year you're spending a lot of time outdoors in the woods, and you may be by yourself. While being alone is great for hunting, it can also be problematic if there's an accident or crisis. In addition to taking basic mundane safety precautions, do this working before you go out to keep yourself free from trouble during a hunt.

Write on the inside of the birch bark three times *I am safe, I am secure, I am protected*. Roll the birch bark into a tube, tie it with the yellow ribbon, and keep it in your vehicle or with your hunting gear.

November 22

Sagittarius
Spell for Efficiency

You'll need:
- Nine index cards and a pen
- A bulletin board

The Zodiac sign of Sagittarius begins on November 22, and this birth sign is often associated with a bit of impatience, a whole lot of drive and motivation, and a need to get things done correctly and efficiently. If you need to become more efficient, take advantage of Sagittarius energy and do this working to help you get your act together.

On each of the index cards, write down one thing you know you've been procrastinating on, something you started and never finished, or a project that is taking entirely too long because your heart just isn't in it. Close your eyes, and say *I will be efficient, I will be proficient. I will get things done, I will finish one by one.*

Organize the cards in order of priority on the bulletin board, with the most important task first. As you accomplish each of them, remove the card, tear it up, and throw it away.

November 23

Spell for Artisanship and Skill

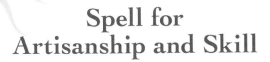

You'll need:
• Ginger root and a cinnamon stick
• A knife
• A gold pouch

If you've been trying to learn a new skill—particularly one of the creative variety—this is a good time of year to hone your craft. Both ginger and cinnamon are considered fiery plants, and they're associated with the ability to develop skills with a bit of practice.

Slice the ginger root into three pieces, and do the same with the cinnamon stick. Place them both in the pouch, and say *With the power and magic these herbs envelop, my abilities grow, my talents develop. Ginger and cinnamon to boost my skill, practice makes perfect, it is my will.*

Keep the pouch near your work area so you can take advantage of the energy of the ginger and cinnamon.

November 24

Cranberry Protection Magic

You'll need:
- Whole uncooked cranberries
- A needle and thread

Cranberries are associated with protection magic, and this time of year you can buy them just about anywhere. When you're doing your holiday grocery shopping, pick up a few extra bags of whole cranberries to work this spell.

String the cranberries along the thread. As you work, say aloud *Protection of my hearth, protection of my home, protection of the ones I love, wherever they may roam.*

As you speak the words, feel the protective energy flowing through your hands and along the string of cranberries. Once you're done, hang them in your home or car for protection. A cranberry garland is very effective dangling from the rearview mirror during your holiday travels.

November 25

Pomegranate Spell for Menopause Symptoms

You'll need:
- A knife
- A pomegranate
- Peppermint tea

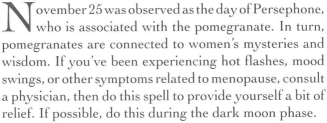

November 25 was observed as the day of Persephone, who is associated with the pomegranate. In turn, pomegranates are connected to women's mysteries and wisdom. If you've been experiencing hot flashes, mood swings, or other symptoms related to menopause, consult a physician, then do this spell to provide yourself a bit of relief. If possible, do this during the dark moon phase.

Slice the pomegranate in half so the seeds are exposed. Scoop out three of them. As you eat the first one, say *One seed, for woman's intuition.* With the second, say *A second seed, for woman's wisdom.* As you eat the third one, say *A third seed, for the privilege and power to which I am entitled.*

Drink the tea, and when you are finished, bury the remainder of the pomegranate in your yard.

November 26

Wishbone
Money Charm

You'll need:
- A wishbone
- Gold paint and a paintbrush
- Dried thyme

This is the season of Thanksgiving, which means at some point you'll probably be near a turkey. This can be very useful if you're magically minded, because a turkey wishbone is a handy tool. While we all know about the tradition of using it to make a wish, you can also use it to draw money into your home during the holiday season. The bigger the turkey, the bigger the wishbone…the bigger the magic!

Coat the wishbone with the gold paint, and then roll it in the thyme leaves so it's covered. Allow it to dry completely, and then hang it up near your front door, saying *Wishbone, wishbone, bringing money in. Wishbone, wishbone, don't let money leave again.*

You may even want to use a second, smaller wishbone to make a charm to tuck in your purse or wallet.

November 27

Threshold Blessing to Welcome Guests

You'll need:
- Pure vanilla extract
- A set of wind chimes

You may notice a significant increase in traffic in your home during the holiday season. From Thanksgiving dinner to Christmas parties to New Year's Eve shenanigans, there's almost always a steady stream of people walking through your front door this time of year. Do this simple threshold blessing spell, on a Thursday if possible, to create a magical welcome for everyone who stops by.

Dip your finger in the vanilla extract, and use it to trace words like WELCOME, FRIENDSHIP, LAUGHTER, and FAMILY on the wind chimes. Hang them beside your front door, saying *Chimes and bells, ringing here, blessings ringing through the year. Welcome friends and family, love and laughter for you and me.*

As your guests stop by to visit, encourage them to tap the wind chimes and make them ring.

November 28

Ancestral Guardian Protection Spell

You'll need:
- Picture frames
- Yellow paint and a paintbrush
- Photos of your deceased ancestors

In many cultures, it is believed that our ancestors watch over us, protecting and guiding us in our day-to-day activities. You can invite your ancestors to keep an eye on your family with this simple spell.

Paint the frames yellow and allow them to dry completely. Put the photos in the frames, and as you do, talk to the people in the pictures. *Aunt Martha, it's so great to see you. Great-grandpa Jim, I'm so glad you're here to watch over us.*

Hang the photos on the wall near your front door, so whenever your family members enter or leave the house, they'll walk past the pictures. Be sure to say hello regularly, and thank them for being household guardians.

Egg Shell
Spell for Shopping
Protection

You'll need:
- A dozen eggshells, rinsed and dried
- White chalk
- Baking soda

In the days following Thanksgiving, many of us start shopping in earnest. With the hectic pace of the holidays, it's easy to get distracted and let down our guard. In many magical traditions, dried and powdered eggshells are used in protection workings. It takes a lot of eggs to make a useful amount of powder, so you can blend the shells with chalk and baking soda.

Use a mortar and pestle to grind the eggshells and chalk into a fine powder. Mix in the baking soda, stirring in a clockwise direction. As you do, say *Protection powder soft and fine, protection for both me and mine.*

Store the blended mixture in a jar with a lid. When you go out shopping, sprinkle a bit in your shoes, your purse, or the trunk of your car to protect your packages.

November 30

Crossroads Spell for Justice

You'll need:
- A white stone
- A black stone
- A blue cloth bag

November 30 is the festival date of the goddess Hecate. She is associated with magic and mystery, as well as divine justice. In particular, she is known as a goddess of the crossroads, and her celebration is the Trivia, meaning *three roads*. If someone has mistreated you and you feel like they haven't gotten their just desserts, do this spell at midnight at a three-way intersection.

Go out at midnight and stand in the center of the crossroads—be sure to watch for traffic before you begin. Hold the white stone in your dominant hand and the black one in the other. Say *I call for justice, as it hasn't yet been done. I call for justice, to right what is wrong. I call for justice, as payment must be made.*

Throw the stones as far away from you as you can. Scoop a bit of dirt from the crossroads and put it in the bag to take home with you. Keep it in a place where you can see it until justice has been served.

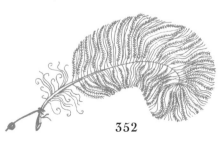

352

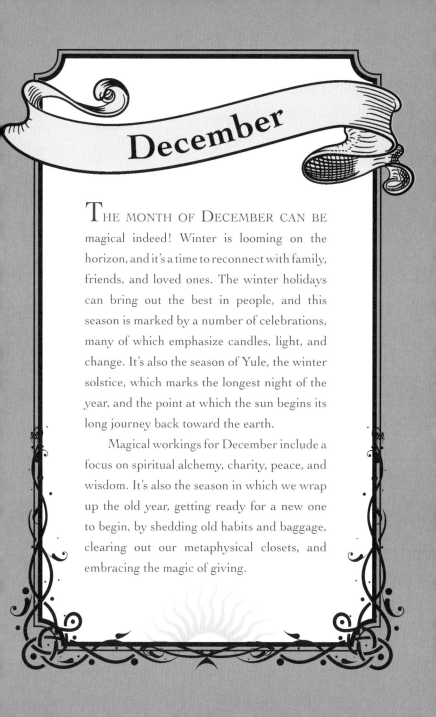

December

THE MONTH OF DECEMBER CAN BE magical indeed! Winter is looming on the horizon, and it's a time to reconnect with family, friends, and loved ones. The winter holidays can bring out the best in people, and this season is marked by a number of celebrations, many of which emphasize candles, light, and change. It's also the season of Yule, the winter solstice, which marks the longest night of the year, and the point at which the sun begins its long journey back toward the earth.

Magical workings for December include a focus on spiritual alchemy, charity, peace, and wisdom. It's also the season in which we wrap up the old year, getting ready for a new one to begin, by shedding old habits and baggage, clearing out our metaphysical closets, and embracing the magic of giving.

December 1

Cinnamon Protection Pinecone Charms

You'll need:
- White glue and a paintbrush
- Pinecones
- A bowl of cinnamon

In some magical folklore, cinnamon is used for protection from evil or negative energies. At this time of year, when the nights are long, cold, and dark, it's not a bad idea to incorporate a bit of magical self-defense into your holiday decorating. The best part about this little craft project? No one will even know that you've placed a magical charm around your home!

Use the brush to dab a bit of glue onto the edges of each pinecone, then roll them in the cinnamon. As you do, say *Protection in the wintertime, protection magic for me and mine. Protection for my house and home, protection for all I call my own.*

Allow the glue to dry, then place the pinecones around your house as a charm of protection. You can even tie a bit of ribbon to them, and hang them on your holiday tree!

December 2

Evergreen Magic for Winter Health

You'll need:
- Three blue candles
- Blue ribbon
- Pine, fir, and holly branches

W hile we're decking our halls with boughs of holly, we're also carrying on a time-honored tradition of bringing seasonal greenery indoors. Evergreens are typically associated with ongoing life and immortality. After all, even though the other trees have lost their leaves by now, the pine and fir are still lush and full of needles. Do this spell to ensure strong health through the holiday season.

Light the candles, and say *Pine and fir and holly green, as the wintertime draws near. Bring us health and happiness, as we close out the year.*

Use the ribbon to tie the branches together, creating a garland. As you do, enjoy the warm, comforting scent of the evergreen boughs. Extinguish the candles, and know that your family will stay well during the hectic holidays.

December 3

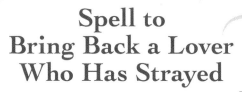

Spell to
Bring Back a Lover
Who Has Strayed

You'll need:
- A red candle
- Frankincense oil
- A photo of your lover

One of the only things worse than ending a relationship is breaking it off right before a major holiday. If your lover has strayed and left you, but you want him or her back in time for the holiday season, early December is the best time to do this working.

Light the candle, and say *Lover come back, this I command. Lover come back to me. Lover come back, by the power of my hand. As I will, so it shall be.*

Dip your finger in the oil, and use it to write the word RETURN on the photo. Finally, drip some of the melted candle wax on the picture in the shape of a heart. Allow the candle to burn out on its own, and hide the photo under your bed until your lover returns.

December 4

Long Nights Moon Spell for Spiritual Alchemy

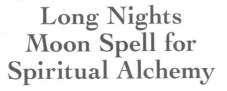

You'll need:
- Three silver candles
- A piece of paper and a pen

December's full moon is called the Long Nights Moon, for obvious reasons. The coming winter solstice is the longest night of the year, and the days are short and chilly. This is a good time to evaluate what you have, count your blessings, and share your good fortune with others. Do this spell, preferably outside, to reach out to others who may be suffering during the winter, either spiritually or physically.

Light the candles, saying *The moon is full above me, the earth is cold beneath me. I have food in my stomach and a warm house to return to. I am healthy and strong. Others are less fortunate, and I show my gratitude by helping where I can.*

Write down three things you are going to do to help other people in your community, such as VOLUNTEER AT THE FOOD PANTRY or COLLECT DONATIONS or even WRITE A CHECK. Fold the paper three times, and drip a bit of wax on the edges to seal it.

Extinguish the candles, and leave the paper where you can see it as a reminder that you have made a commitment to help others.

December 5

Gingerbread Men
Prosperity Poppets

You'll need:
- Your favorite gingerbread recipe and ingredients
- Gingerbread man cookie cutters
- Grated orange peel
- Cinnamon sugar

Many magical traditions use poppets, or dolls, as a way of performing magic. The poppet is often designed to represent a person; usually it is made from cloth or some other sort of fabric. Poppets can be used for all kinds of things, from healing magic to love spells. Seeing as it's December, why not make gingerbread men poppets to bring prosperity into your home for the holidays?

Prepare your gingerbread men according to the recipe. Before you put them in the oven, sprinkle them with the grated orange peel and cinnamon sugar. As you do, say *Prosperity and abundance, for my family. Abundance and prosperity, for my home.*

Bake the gingerbread men, allow them to cool as directed, and place them around your home to welcome magical abundance during the winter holiday season.

December 6

Holiday Gift Wrap Blessing Magic

You'll need:
- Wrapping paper
- Scissors and tape
- Sandalwood oil

From St. Nicholas to Odin, this time of year is one of legendary figures leaving gifts for us. If you're doing a gift exchange with friends or family, you can sneak a little magic into the wrapping paper, offering the blessings you wish for them as part of the gift. Use gift wrap with a busy, colorful pattern or design.

Before you wrap each gift, cut off the appropriate amount of paper from the roll. Dip your finger in the oil, and on the inside of the paper, use a very light touch to write what you wish for the recipient, such as PROSPERITY, FINANCIAL SUCCESS, or TRUE LOVE. After you've written the words, allow the paper to dry for a moment, then wrap the gift.

December 7

Mistletoe
Fertility Magic

You'll need:
- A pink candle
- Dried mistletoe, ivy, and patchouli
- A cloth drawstring bag

Mistletoe is everywhere during the holidays, and if you're really lucky, you might just get a kiss while you're standing beneath it. In addition to romance and peace, mistletoe is connected to fertility magic. If you're having trouble conceiving, see a medical professional, then make this sachet to help increase your chances at fertility. Try to do this working on a Thursday during the most fertile part of your cycle.

Light the candle, place the herbs inside the bag, and pull the drawstring tight. Say *I have so much love to give, and so much love to share. So much room in my heart and home, so much room to care.*

Extinguish the candle, and place the bag under your mattress.

December 8

Instant
Karma Spell

You'll need:
- A compact mirror
- A marker
- A photo of the person who has insulted you

In classical mythology, Astraea was the virginal daughter of Zeus, and was associated with justice and righteous indignation. If someone has offended or insulted you without cause, this simple spell will send back what the individual has dished out.

Open the mirror, and write back at you across it. Hold up the mirror so the photo is reflected in it, and say *What you send to me bounces back to you. Your harmful words and hateful deeds return back to you. Your anger and insults I send back to you.*

Snap the mirror shut, with the photo inside it, and say *When you apologize and make amends, I release you from this spell.*

Keep the photo inside the compact until the person makes amends. Then open the compact, remove the photo, and clean off the mirror.

December 9

Candy Cane
Love Spell

You'll need:
- Two candy canes
- A pink ribbon

Peppermint is associated with love, lust, and passion. If you're looking for love magic, a candy cane is a powerful tool indeed. Use this spell to bring love your way when you don't have a specific someone in mind.

Hold the candy canes together, and beginning at the bottoms, slowly use the ribbon to bind them together. As you wrap the ribbon around the candy canes, say three times *Holiday lights and holiday blessings, love please come to be. The season of joy and season of peace, I want someone to share it with me.*

Once you've wrapped the ribbon all the way around the hook of the candy canes, secure it and hang them up in your home to invite love into your life.

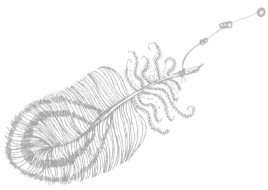

December 10

Spell to Handle a Workplace Bully

You'll need:
- A black candle
- A photo of the bully
- A pair of tweezers

It's hard to believe that there are adult bullies, but they exist, and you might work with one. If a bully at work is harassing you—or a coworker is being victimized—it's time to put an end to the problem.

Light the candle and say *[NAME], you are no more. You are not worth my time or energy. You will now leave me alone.*

Tear off a small piece of the photo. Using the tweezers, hold it into the candle flame until it burns away. As it does, say *[NAME], goodbye. You are no more.* Continue doing this, with small bits of the photo, until there is nothing left but ashes and dust. Extinguish the candle, and go enjoy your day at work.

December 11

Turquoise Spell
to Establish Peace

You'll need:
- Turquoise
- Lavender oil
- A piece of blue cloth

December's birthstone is turquoise, which is associated with reconciling, mending quarrels, and establishing peaceful solutions to problems. December is a month of peace and love — or at least it should be — so if you've been quarreling with someone, now is your chance to mend the rift. No matter whose fault it may have been originally, it's time to let bygones be bygones.

Hold the turquoise and think about the other person involved in the disagreement. Don't worry about who started it; what matters is that you're willing to end it. Say *Hard feelings be gone, over and done. Peace and friendship, unite us as one. Mend what's broken, between you and me. As I will, so it shall be.*

Put a bit of the lavender oil on the cloth, and wrap it around the turquoise. Next time you see the person, offer it as a gift.

December 12

Spell to Cut Down on Holiday Overindulgence

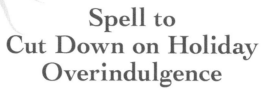

You'll need:
- A symbol of whatever your weakness is
- A black garbage bag
- Your trash can

It happens every year. We eat way too much at the office holiday party and feel miserable for days, or we drink a little more than we should at Grandma's Christmas dinner celebration. While it's easy to tell ourselves to relax, because after all, it is the holiday season, the fact is sometimes we just feel terrible and guilty afterward. Rather than regretting our overindulgence after the fact, we can use magic to keep it from happening in the first place.

If you know your bad habit is overeating, use some type of food—a bag of chips, a piece of cake—as your symbol. If you're worried about nipping a bit too much wine, use a wine bottle, and so forth. Place the symbol into the garbage bag. Tie the top of the bag in three knots, and go outside to your trash can.

Hold the trash bag with both hands, at the knots, and begin swinging it over your head in a circle, moving in a counterclockwise direction. As you swing, say *Over my head, over and done, I'm so over you*, three times. After the third time, drop it in your trash can, go back inside, and forget about it.

December 13

Sweet Vanilla Love Jar

You'll need:
- A cup of sugar
- A jar with a lid
- A vanilla bean, chopped in three pieces

Vanilla beans are associated with love and harmony, so why not use them in magic? You can combine a vanilla bean with a jar of sugar to help facilitate harmonious love energy between the people who live in your home. This is the season of gift giving, so you can either create this love jar to use in your own house, or dress it up with a pretty ribbon to give to someone else whose home might benefit from it.

Pour the sugar into the jar, and add the vanilla bean pieces. Place the lid on the jar, and swirl it around so the vanilla blends with the sugar, saying *Love and sweetness in our life, love and sweetness, no more strife. Love and sweetness between you and me, as I will, so it shall be.*

Keep the jar someplace your family spends a lot of time, like in the kitchen or near the fireplace.

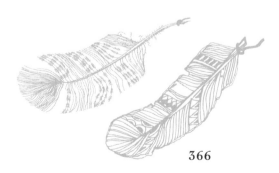

December 14

Yule Log
Spell to Burn
Your Troubles Away

You'll need:
- A Yule log
- Paper and pens
- A fireplace

It's a custom in many places to make a Yule log, decorated with symbols of the season. You can create one fairly easily: arrange ivy, pinecones, candles, and ribbons around a plain log. Generally, it's a tradition to burn the Yule log each December, saving a bit of the ashes for the following year. If you have a fireplace or a fire pit, you can do a Yule log spell to burn away your troubles as the year winds down.

Give each family member a piece of paper, and ask everyone to write down problems they would like to be free of in the coming year. When they have finished, roll up the papers and tuck them into the greenery and ribbons on the Yule log. Place the log in the fireplace and get a good blaze going. Watch as your troubles burn away and are carried up the chimney and out of your life.

December 15

Spell to
Get Loaned Money
Back

You'll need:
- A green candle
- A piece of paper and a pen

If you've ever loaned money to a friend, you probably knew there was a possibility you'd never see it again. However, you may need that money, especially around the holidays. Do this working to nudge the borrower into repaying the loan, even if it's only an installment.

Light the candle, and say *A loan of money in faith was made, now to satisfy, it must be paid.*

Write on the piece of paper as though it was a check made out to you from the person who borrowed money. Be sure to specify the full dollar amount. Say *What's owed will soon come back to me, as I will, so it shall be.*

Fold up the paper and keep it in your wallet or purse to draw the money back to you.

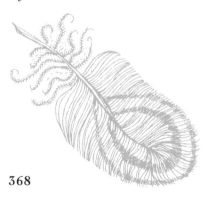

December 16

Winter
Travel Spell

You'll need:
- Three iron nails
- A yellow cloth bag
- A chip of asphalt from your own driveway or parking spot

More people travel at this time of year than any other, so if you're loading up the family to go on a holiday road trip, do a bit of magic before your departure. In addition to mundane, common-sense practices like checking your oil and tires before you leave, this will help you avoid car troubles and get everyone there safe and sound.

Put the nails in the bag, saying *Iron for protection, to keep my family safe as we travel far and wide.* Add the asphalt, and say *This asphalt is my home, and my car shall return to park on it unharmed.* Put the bag in the trunk of your car, near the spare tire, and don't remove it until you get back home.

December 17

Spell for an
Amazing Holiday Party

You'll need:
• A purple candle
• A bag of individually wrapped holiday candies
• A festive bowl or candy dish

December 17 was the date of the annual Saturnalia festival, which was chock-full of merrymaking, party, and general debauchery. If you're hosting a holiday party and you're anxious about whether it will be a success, do this spell the morning of your event, at sunrise.

Light the candle, and pour the candies into the bowl. Hold them up to the candle, and say *Success and triumph will come tonight, my holiday gathering will go just right. Friends and family, joy and fun, a good time will be had by everyone!*

Let the candle burn until the party begins. When your guests arrive, extinguish the candle and offer everyone candies from the bowl.

December 18

Spell to Make Yourself Irresistible

You'll need:
- A pink candle
- Rose oil
- A magnet

It's the holiday season, and a time of year when we all want to feel good about ourselves. The better our self-image, the more appealing other people tend to find us—and when others find us attractive, it boosts our self-image. You can give this cycle a bit of a jump-start with this simple spell. Do this working in front of your mirror before you go to a big holiday event, like a concert or a party. Get dressed up in your nicest clothes so you can really turn some heads.

Light the candle, and look in the mirror. Say *I'm simply irresistible. I'm simply amazing. I'm simply desirable. I'm simply awesome.*

Dab a bit of the rose oil on your wrists and at the base of your throat, and then add a bit to the magnet. Extinguish the candle, and drop the magnet in your purse to attract people to you at the gathering.

December 19

Spell to Send a Message in Your Dreams

You'll need:
- A silver candle
- A pen
- A photo of the person
- Lavender

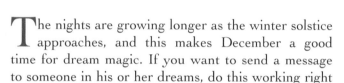

The nights are growing longer as the winter solstice approaches, and this makes December a good time for dream magic. If you want to send a message to someone in his or her dreams, do this working right before you go to bed, preferably on a Monday night.

Light the candle, and say *[*NAME*], I send a message to you in my dreams. Words I cannot speak in waking hours come to you in sleep.*

Write your message on the person's photo, and tuck it, along with the lavender, under your pillow. Extinguish the candle, and think about your message as you fall asleep.

December 20

Winter Solstice
Spell to Welcome the Sun

You'll need:
- A gold candle
- A cup of hot tea

Yule, the winter solstice, takes place around December 20 each year. This is the point in the year when the sun begins making its long journey back toward earth. After the solstice, the days slowly begin to get longer again. Do this spell outdoors at dawn on the solstice to welcome the sun's return.

Stand so you're facing east, and light the candle as the sun begins to break on the horizon. Say *As the wheel of the year turns, light returns. The light of the sun comes back to us, bringing life and warmth with it. The shadows will vanish, and life will continue. The light of the sun blesses us once more.*

Raise your cup in a toast to the sun, and once it has completely risen, drink your tea and enjoy the sunlight.

December 21

Spell to Get Along With Relatives

You'll need:
- A blue candle
- Basil

During the holiday season, everyone's stress level gets a little higher than usual, and even family members that we love can get on our last nerves. If you're spending the holidays with extended family or your partner's relatives, do this working before any get-togethers take place.

Light the candle, and scatter the basil around it in a circle. Say *Peace be with us, as we gather together. Peace be with us, now and forever. Joined by the bonds of family, peace and love for you and me.*

Extinguish the candle, and sprinkle the basil into your shoes before you go off to your family gathering.

December 22

Capricorn Spell for Self Discipline

You'll need:
- A purple candle
- A poinsettia plant
- A black marker

The Zodiac sign of Capricorn begins on December 22, and this birth sign is typically associated with planning, orderliness, organization, and being supremely focused on completing the task at hand. If you need a bit more self-discipline in your life, do this spell to help you get back on track.

Light the candle, and say *I am focused, I am disciplined, I am orderly.* Pluck three leaves from the poinsettia, and on them write the words PLAN, EXECUTE, and COMPLETE.

Say *In all my tasks and challenges, I will craft a plan ahead of time. I will execute my plans, and I will complete my undertakings to the best of my abilities.*

Extinguish the candle, and carry the leaves in your pocket or keep them at your desk at work.

December 23

A Spell to
Get Some Alone Time

You'll need:
- Bergamot
- A white candle
- A quartz crystal

The holiday season is a nonstop barrage of social interaction, from family and friends dropping by to office gift exchanges, and it can be emotionally exhausting. If you find yourself stressing out and can't seem to get a moment to yourself, do this working to get a bit of alone time.

Go in your bathroom and fill the tub with warm water. Add the bergamot, light the candle, and climb into the tub. Close your eyes, holding the crystal in your hands. Say *No one can see me, no one will bother me, this time is mine alone. I am invisible, I am unseen, this time is mine alone. I embrace my solitude, I embrace my peace, this time is mine alone.*

Relax in your warm bath until the water cools, then extinguish the candle.

December 24

Sun Spell for Energy

You'll need:
- A yellow or an orange candle
- A zircon stone set in a piece of jewelry

This was the time of year for the festival of Sol Invictus, which honored the power and energy of the sun god. If you're feeling run-down from holiday stress, get outside, catch a few rays, and do this working to rejuvenate yourself.

Go to a place where you won't be bothered, and light the candle. Hold it up to the sun and say *The day is cold but the sun is out. Fire in the sky, fire in my blood, fire in my heart. I absorb the energy and power of the sun, and it revitalizes my spirit.*

Hold up the zircon jewelry so the sun's rays are reflected in the stone. Move it back and forth to create a bouncing ray of light. Say *The sun is high, it is in my blood, it is in my heart. I carry the energy and power of the sun with me, to revitalize my spirit.*

Extinguish the candle, and wear the jewelry as you go about your day.

December 25

Spell to Get
Into the Holiday Spirit

You'll need:
- Peppermint oil
- A red candle
- Three holiday chocolates

The winter holidays can be tough for some people, and whether you're celebrating Christmas, Hanukkah, or the winter solstice, there are times when you're just not feeling that holly-jolly spirit. Do this working to boost your mood so you can enjoy the season of joy and peace.

Brush a light coating of the peppermint oil on the candle, and light it. Close your eyes, and think about all the blessings you have in your life at this time of year. Consider your family, your friends, your health, and all the other things you have to feel joyous about. Say *It is the season of love, the season of peace, the season of joy. I welcome the holiday spirit into my heart, because I have so many blessings. I welcome happiness into my heart, because I am so fortunate. I welcome love into my heart, because I am surrounded by it each day.*

Slowly eat the chocolates, and as you do, think about love, peace, and joy. Allow the candle to burn out on its own, and go celebrate your holiday.

December 26

Spell to
Prevent an Argument

You'll need:
- An envelope
- A blue marker or pen
- Equal parts chamomile, lavender, and St. John's wort

In the mythology of Wales, the Cŵn Annwn are the mystical hounds of the underworld, and they hunt in late December, spreading chaos and discord throughout the land. If your life is a bit hectic right now, and you feel like every conversation turns into a disagreement, do this spell ahead of time to prevent arguments and conflicts from occurring.

On the envelope, write the words PEACE, HARMONY, AGREEMENT three times each. Add the herbs, and seal the envelope, saying *Peace will reign supreme today, harmony as all get along. Agreement will come before arguments start, and nothing will go wrong.*

Tuck the envelope in your pocket, and carry it as you go about your day and interact with others.

December 27

Winter Blessings Divination Spell

You'll need:
• Four stones or tiles,
painted red, green, white, and gold
• A cloth bag

In many European magical traditions, winter is a prime time for shamanic journeys and divination. You can do your own divination to see what the coming year holds for you, so you know what you have to look forward to.

Place the stones or tiles in the bag, and close your eyes. Say *The old year is ending, and blessings counted. The new year is coming, with blessings to be welcomed. Reveal to me what is in store.*

Reach into the bag and draw a single stone. Each color has a different meaning:

RED: *Good luck, passion, and love*

GREEN: *Fertility and abundance*

WHITE: *Purification, peace, and spiritual development*

GOLD: *Power, energy, and prosperity*

No matter which one is revealed to you, take a moment to show gratitude for your blessings.

December 28

Spell to Help
a Friend in Trouble

You'll need:
- A pickle
- A glass jar with a lid
- Honey

Ever have a friend or family member in trouble? Sometimes people we love get into a jam, and there's not much we can do except be there when they need us. Whatever kind of entanglement your friend has gotten into, after you've offered mundane help, add a bit of magic to help alleviate the situation.

Put the pickle in the jar, and say *[NAME], you may be in trouble, but I know you well. I will be there for you, through thick and thin. I am here to help you always, and we will get through this side by side, hand in hand.*

Add the honey to the jar, and say *[NAME], when things get bad, they will always get better. When things are hard, they will always get easier. When things are sour, they will always get sweeter. I am here for you when you need me.*

Put the lid on the jar, and store it somewhere in your home until your friend's troubles have passed.

December 29

End-of-Year
Money Magic Spell

You'll need:
- A fillable glass ornament
- Green tissue paper, torn into pieces
- Allspice, grated orange peel, and pine needles

The holiday season is winding down, and many of us could use a bit of extra cash to pay off those end-of-year bills. Do this working to bring some extra money your way.

Open the ornament, and fill it with bits of tissue paper. As you do, say *Green is the color of money, green money come my way. Green to help with the holidays, because I've got bills to pay.*

Add the allspice, orange peel, and pine needles, and close up the ornament. Hang it on a ribbon in your home to draw in money.

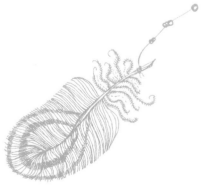

December 30

A Spell to Break the Ice

You'll need:
- Nine ice cubes
- A pan
- A lemon

If you're attending any parties this time of year, chances are good you're going to meet people you've never encountered. If you're shy—or you just never know what you're supposed to say—do this working before you go to a party.

Place the ice cubes in the pan, on your stovetop, and turn the heat to low. As the ice cubes begin to melt, cut the lemon into nine pieces. Add them into the melting ice one at a time, saying *Easy friendship, breaking the ice, getting to know you would be nice. Barriers down, new friends for me, as I will, so it shall be.*

Once the ice has melted completely, turn off the burner. Get dressed up, go to the party, and have a good time with new people.

December 31

Spell to
End the Old Year

You'll need:
- Your favorite fireworks*
- A pen

I t's the end of the calendar year, which means new beginnings are right around the corner. But before we can get started on new endeavors, we have to say farewell to the old ones. Now is your chance to eliminate everything from the past year that didn't work out for you. After all, tomorrow everything begins anew. Do this working just before midnight on New Year's Eve.

On the fireworks, write what you want to eliminate, such as BAD DEBT, UNHEALTHY RELATIONSHIPS, or POOR JUDGMENT. once you've noted everything—and you can use multiple fireworks if you need to—say *The old year has ended, and I say farewell. These are the things that will no longer drag me down. I send them away, never to return.*

Light the fireworks (using proper safety precautions), step back, and watch all your bad stuff shoot off into the night.

* Be sure to follow all local regulations regarding the use of fireworks.

Patti Wigington has been practicing as a Pagan since 1987. She is a High Priestess in her home state of Ohio, and is the founder of Clan of the Stone Circle, a Celtic Pagan tradition. In 2007, Patti joined About.com as the Paganism & Wicca Expert. In addition to her work for About, Patti has written several novels and a children's book, and has contributed to numerous anthologies.

You can find Patti online at
www.pattiwigington.com.